THE NEW YORK TIMES
Book of Trees and Shrubs

Edited by Joan Lee Faust

THE NEW YORK TIMES GARDEN BOOK

THE NEW YORK TIMES BOOK OF HOME LANDSCAPING

THE NEW YORK TIMES BOOK OF LAWN CARE

THE NEW YORK TIMES BOOK OF TREES AND SHRUBS

These are BORZOI BOOKS *published in New York by* ALFRED A. KNOPF

The New York Times
BOOK OF TREES
AND SHRUBS

Edited by JOAN LEE FAUST

NEW YORK : *Alfred·A·Knopf*

1 9 6 7

L. C. catalog card number: 64–12303

THIS IS A BORZOI BOOK,
PUBLISHED BY ALFRED A. KNOPF, INC.

PUBLISHED MAY 15, 1964
SECOND PRINTING, JANUARY 1965
THIRD PRINTING, NOVEMBER 1967

Contents

THE NEW YORK TIMES
Book of Trees and Shrubs

AS THE ARTIST seeks from a palette the colors for his canvas, so the gardener selects from innumerable kinds of trees and shrubs those plants that will make his landscape beautiful. Great changes are taking place in the garden world. No longer are the out-sized plants that soon overtake the property selected for homes. Tidy, slow-growing shrubs are winning appeal. Evergreens, for year-round effect, are dominating the landscapes. Trees and shrubs with interesting form and good flower colors are coming to the fore. The mood of the times is dictating this. Low, spreading homes, compact suburban communities and numerous demands on leisure time are creating a need for plants that are decorative yet easy to maintain.

Many of the newer forms of these plants are scarce during the first few years following their introduction and gardeners often have to search for them. Prices, too, may be a bit higher. But as long as gardeners are discriminating in their plant selections, they will find their efforts rewarded in worthwhile dividends—low-upkeep gardens with distinction and individuality the year through.

Texture contrasts are achieved by blending the foliage of pachysandra and rhododendron with the white bark of the birch trees for accent.

Paul E. Genereux

Landscaping with Trees and Shrubs

ALICE RECKNAGEL IREYS

KNOWLEDGE of plant scale, form, texture and color and an understanding of the basic principles of landscape design, including proportion, unity, balance and rhythm, work together to guide the planning of a composition whether it be a foundation planting, boundary screening or self-contained garden. Plants are forever changing, not only in size, but with the seasons, so a comprehensive mental picture of each plant should be part of the equipment of every landscape planner.

The scale of a plant may be described as the relative size as it relates to surroundings. Trees may be selected to frame a house, give shade to a terrace or hide an objectionable view. The variety selected depends upon the size of the house. For example, a large elm suits a Georgian house while a flowering crabapple may be more fitting for a low Cape Cod cottage.

Moreover, the form that a tree or shrub assumes must be recognized before it can be used to best advantage. There are many shapes to be found in ornamentals: the stately v-shape of the elm, the domelike form of the beech or horsechestnut, the pyramid of the firs, hemlocks and hollies and the weeping aspect of the willows. Plant selection depends upon the particular spot and the form that is best for it.

Another important factor to consider is the utilization of plant texture. The size of the leaves and how they are attached to the stem and the surface quality of the foliage, whether it is rough or smooth, dull or shiny, thick or thin, are key qualities to admire. Foliage texture of plants can create many moods and can give a landscape composition a sense of movement and lightness. Among trees, for example, the oak suggests a strong tree because of the heavy texture of its bark and leaves, while the honey locust offers grace and lightness.

Color compositions are usually determined by the color of the

An overgrown foundation planting hides the charm and architectural design of the house. *Gottscho-Schleisner*

foliage, which is affected by the texture of the leaves. Trees with many leaves close together will appear as one color, while those that have more open foliage will be spotted with shadows and appear as two colors. The color range of greens is tremendous. Notice, for example, the various greens that one sees in the different viburnums and dogwoods. A landscape planned with consideration of foliage colors will make strong impressions.

For bloom, there is a wide range of flowering trees and shrubs

Full-sized rhododendrons block the front windows of a Colonial house. These mature specimens could be moved to the rear garden and could be replaced by smaller-growing species. *Gottscho-Schleisner*

from which to choose. Here it is necessary to select carefully plants that have harmonious flower colors. The flower tones of azaleas can portray a fascinating picture, if matched properly. For example, the flame, bronze, orange and buff varieties all blend to form a pleasing setting.

When the scale, form, texture and color of the plants is established, then the basic factors of good design can be incorporated. Proportion, which is an underlying principle of all art, is more important to landscape development. Along with scale and form, it helps the gardener to select the right plant for the right place. For example, hollies and small-leaved rhododendrons are adapted to a small garden. Their proportion is pleasing and the plants have the proper relationship to each other and to the setting.

Unity in planting composition is a means of pulling plants together so that one will not be distracted by the great variety. A nursery, which is a fascinating place to visit, does not ever give a unified picture. A garden or boundary planting must never have such a hodge-podge variety of plants that the eye is never satisfied but moves from plant to plant.

Balance gives equilibrium and stability. If trees and shrubs are arranged around a central feature or an axis, they will have symmetrical balance. An asymmetrical balance is most often used for informal designs. A large tree may be placed on one side of the garden and balanced by a group of low-spreading yews.

Rhythm can be found in the repetition of the same plant to give

A well-selected grouping of deciduous and evergreen shrubs hems the terrace and lends to the perennial plantings along the stone fence.

Paul E. Genereux

a feeling of movement. In small back yards it is possible to repeat at regular intervals a few dogwood trees. This gives a sense of progression so that one's eyes are lead to a focal point. Always remember to select plants that have the same quality of texture in order to achieve unity and harmony. Never use a large number of different plants but repeat the same plant groups often.

Perhaps one species can dominate the composition. For example, in a boundary planting, it might be advantageous to select one or two summering-flowering trees and shrubs. The main part of the plan would then be developed with some needled evergreens and a few broadleaved types. Thus the planting will have variety of bloom, texture and foliage color.

In summary, the four following rules may be helpful to use when planning a home landscape design:

1. STUDY: the design of the property as a whole; the need for evergreens and deciduous masses of varying heights and spread; the requirements for screen planting to hide objectionable views.

2. SELECT PLANT MATERIALS: to fit into the general design; to form proper and interesting landscape compositions.

3. OBSERVE: the climatic requirements; shade, sun or soil requirements; general plant surroundings in the neighborhood.

4. CONSIDER: the cost of the planting and future maintenance. If a budget is necessary, a plan will allow the work to progress in stages and the completed job will have a unified appearance.

2

Plant Hardiness

FRANCIS DE VOS

THE hardiness of a plant is its inherent ability to withstand low temperatures. The average annual minimum temperature of an area, more than any other factor, determines whether a plant will survive.

This rule of thumb applies to Florida and Southern California as much as to the Northern states. Tropical plants may endure cold injury even when the temperature is above freezing, while plants of the tundra may not be damaged until the thermometer reaches 60 degrees below zero. Freezing injury, winter burn, heaving and bark splitting are the most common types of cold damage experienced in gardens.

Injury or death of plant cells that follows exposure to freezing temperatures is not a temperature effect per se, but it is caused by ice formation within (or between) the cells. Ice formation within cells causes irreversible changes in the living matter (protoplasm) of the cells. Most plant losses by freezing are attributed to this type of injury. Ice formation between cells may not be injurious.

Loss of a plant from freezing injury depends on the extent and the kinds of tissue involved. Injury to the roots or the main stem or trunk at or near the ground level may result in loss of all above-ground parts or the entire plant. The killing-back of portions of twigs and branches is the most common type of freezing injury.

The browning of broadleaved evergreens and conifers during winter is commonly called winter burn. Conditions conducive to severe winter burn are frozen soil, low moisture supply in the soil, strong constant winds and bright warm sun. A dry fall coupled with a constantly or intermittently frozen soil sets the stage for winter burn.

If plants are exposed to strong winds or direct sun, or both, their leaves lose water faster than it can be replaced by the roots in frozen or cold soil. Plants in full winter sun are damaged more than those in shade. Water loss is greatly accelerated by high leaf temperatures, which may reach 80 degrees when the air temperature is below 32 degrees.

The alternate thawing and freezing of the top layer of soil frequently heaves young plants out of the soil or breaks the root-soil contacts of recently transplanted plants. Plants so affected dry out and die back to ground level or are killed.

Differential heating and cooling of the bark of some trees and shrubs results in stresses which cause the bark to split and crack. Young azaleas and boxwoods not completely hardened and plants of borderline hardiness are particularly susceptible. Frequently this injury is not noticed until the dying back of branches or of the entire plant during the late spring or summer.

The degree to which a plant can become hardened to low temperatures depends largely on its inherent ability to respond to environmental conditions that tend to increase frost resistance. Some plants are incapable of being hardened by any known treatment.

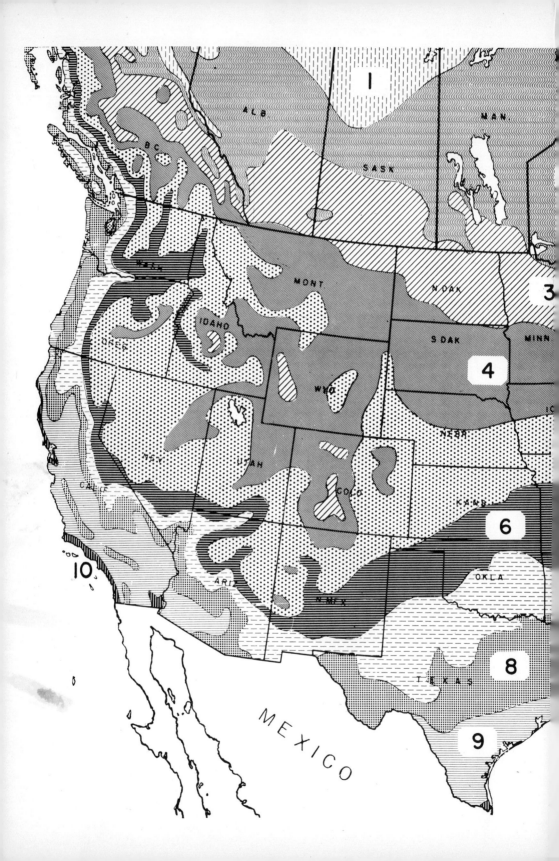

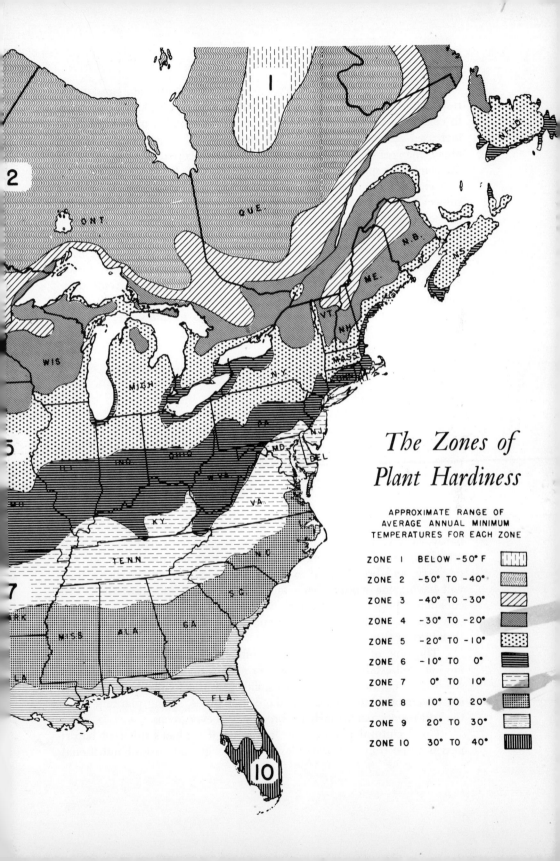

The Zones of Plant Hardiness

APPROXIMATE RANGE OF
AVERAGE ANNUAL MINIMUM
TEMPERATURES FOR EACH ZONE

ZONE 1	BELOW −50° F	
ZONE 2	−50° TO −40°	
ZONE 3	−40° TO −30°	
ZONE 4	−30° TO −20°	
ZONE 5	−20° TO −10°	
ZONE 6	−10° TO 0°	
ZONE 7	0° TO 10°	
ZONE 8	10° TO 20°	
ZONE 9	20° TO 30°	
ZONE 10	30° TO 40°	

The seasonal changes that occur in the temperate zone are largely responsible for the annual increase and decrease in a plant's resistance to cold. The decreasing day length and cooler nights of fall result in increased resistance by causing a cessation of growth and bringing about changes in the physical and chemical properties of cells. With the coming of spring, nearly all frost resistance is lost.

The hardening and dehardening processes are gradual and are subject to climatic changes that are seldom of the same magnitude or in the same sequence from year to year. It is, therefore, virtually impossible to say how hardy any particular plant is at any given time.

In the disastrous spring freeze of 1955 in the Southeast, half-century-old azaleas were killed after coming into active growth. In the fall of the same year in the Pacific Northwest a sudden extreme drop in temperature after a mild fall was equally disastrous. In both cases, plants which had survived lower temperatures in midwinter of other years succumbed at higher temperatures when in an incomplete state of hardiness.

The gardener's first line of defense against winter damage should be the selection of plants to be grown. In most plant groups, some species and varieties are tougher and hardier than others.

Reputable nurserymen, landscape architects, plant societies, state agricultural schools, botanical gardens and arboretums can assist in making selections. Also, the Plant Hardiness Zone Map, reproduced on pages 10–11, is a helpful planting guide. It shows the average annual minimum temperatures of the ten zones of the United States. Separate copies in color can be ordered from the Superintendent of Documents, Washington, D.C., 20025.

Satisfactory performance is not guaranteed even from a cold-hardy variety. The gardener still must use his judgment. The hardiest plants should be given the most exposed or coldest site on the property, and broadleaved evergreens should be planted where they will have some winter shade and be protected from the wind. The common experience, particularly with borderline-hardy species, is that one-year-old plants are more difficult to bring through the first winter than two- or three-year-old plants.

The time of planting can also influence the results. Plants which are not well established when winter arrives may be heaved from the soil or may not be able to absorb sufficient water to offset the desiccating effects of winter winds. In the colder states, spring planting gives the best results, particularly for broadleaved evergreens.

Good cultural practices are necessary if a plant's inherent hardiness is to be fully realized. Plants of low vigor because of nutritional deficiencies, poor soil drainage, and insect or disease damage are less likely to endure the rigors of winter weather than healthy plants. At the other extreme, plants with vigorous soft growth produced as the result of late-summer applications of nitrogen fertilizer do not have time to mature and harden; thus they are also highly susceptible to cold injury.

Since winter injury, particularly to broadleaved evergreens, is usually more severe under conditions of low soil moisture, plants should be watered even during the winter if drought is severe. Watering is especially important to plants deprived of rainfall because they are growing near the house foundation or under a roof overhang; they frequently are killed by cold temperatures and drying winds aggravated by the dry soil.

Of equal importance to over-wintering of plants is soil drainage. Heaving is more common in waterlogged soils than in well-drained soils. The active and extensive root system developed by a plant in well-drained soil is the best insurance against the drying effects of freezing temperatures and winds.

A three- to four-inch soil mulch of leaves, wood chips, well-decayed sawdust or pine needles is generally considered to be effective in reducing heaving caused by alternate freezing and thawing of the soil surface. A snow mulch is equally effective but cannot be depended on in many areas. Soils beneath mulches do not freeze deeply or at all, thereby keeping soil moisture more available to the plants.

Recent experiments have indicated that bark splitting of azaleas growing in open fields can be prevented by removing the mulch in fall before freezing weather sets in. The reason is that the temperature above a mulch may be as much as five to six degrees lower than over adjacent bare soil because the mulch prevents the radiation of heat from the soil to the surrounding air. Additional experiments are needed to determine whether the procedure is applicable to azaleas and other woody plants growing in home landscapes.

In recent years, plastic-type sprays called anti-desiccants have been introduced to prevent winter burn. Reports indicate that they are effective when applied in late autumn. These sprays, however, should not be considered a substitute for the selection of hardy varieties or the observance of good cultural practices.

Acclimatization is defined as the natural process by which organisms become adapted to a climate at first harmful. In its narrowest sense, it refers only to heritable changes that occur in the course of generations. Horticulturally speaking, the term is used more loosely; it generally refers to any change following transplanting that enables the plant to become established in its new environment. There is no evidence to support the idea that a plant's genetically based hardiness will be increased by exposing the plant to two or three winters in a colder climate.

The principal adjustment that a plant makes during the acclimatization period is developing an extensive root system. This is no small matter, however, since much of the winter injury is directly related to water loss. Thus it is obvious that the selection of cold-hardy species and varieties and the application of good cultural practices are the keys to winter survival and vigor of many kinds of plants in the garden.

3

Pruning Deciduous Shrubs

KENNETH MEYER

SHRUBS are always more attractive and considerably more effective when they are kept free of dead wood and are neat and trim. This is accomplished largely by pruning at the right time and in the proper way. Proper pruning of deciduous shrubs calls for some accurate knowledge of each plant's habit of growth and time of blooming. Lacking it, most men are likely to commit a kind of shrub butchery with the pruning shears, while the average woman gardener will prune with such hesitancy that the results will often be futile and inadequate.

A good rule to follow is to trim out branches or shoots only when there is sound reason for doing so. Dead branches or shoots, of course, are removed without hesitation. Also, those severely infested with scale insects or disease call for drastic treatment. Beyond this point, consider carefully before pruning. It is easy to mar the natural form and beauty of a shrub by giving it a general trimming instead of a judicious thinning out of old wood, which stimulates young growth.

As a general rule, deciduous shrubs should not be pruned too severely at any one time. Also, it is undesirable to cut back strong growth only at the top. This gives the bushes a de-horned appearance in winter, lacking grace and attractiveness. Shearing is to be avoided. It is best to reach into the bush and trim out old branches and shoots at the base, enabling new growth to get more light. Avoid ugly stubs by cutting above a node or leaf joint. The amount of wood to be removed naturally varies with the number of new branches and shoots the shrub has produced.

Forsythia, for example, looks unnatural and unattractive when trimmed with a flat top or in a rigid crew-cut fashion. Forsythia grows openly and gracefully. Plants, however, do require rather severe yearly pruning to maintain a tidy appearance and to keep them from spreading too rampantly. This is best done immediately after flowering. The oldest stalks, which have already bloomed, should be cut almost to ground level to allow young new growth to take their place. All weak shoots and poorly placed branches should be removed. Such procedures enable the plant to blossom freely on gracefully arching branches, rather than flower sparsely on old growth. This same method of pruning is applicable to many other well-known shrubs, among them flowering quince, early-blooming spireas, weigelas, deutzias, kerria, lilacs and mock oranges. The lovely *Viburnum carlesi* may also be pruned the same way.

The best time to prune deciduous shrubs depends, as a rule, on their flowering habits. Those which bloom on new growth in late spring or summer are pruned in late winter or very early spring. Abelia is an example, as are buddleia, hypericum, clethra, crape myrtle and the late flowering spireas. Those shrubs which flower on the previous year's wood should be pruned soon after they have finished blooming. This prevents formation of seed pods and also conserves the plant's vitality. This category includes magnolias, azaleas, broom, pearl bush and most climbing roses. A few kinds benefit by a light pruning immediately after flowering and again in early spring. Examples of this are lonicera, *Viburnum opulus* and *V. tomentosum*.

Some shrubs may be encouraged to bloom almost continuously by judicious pruning. Weigelas, some of the buddleias and spirea Anthony Waterer, when cut back immediately after one crop of flowers, will often bloom again. Strong growth should be headed in and some branches pruned back. In a few weeks the strongest growth may be cut again and a scattering of bloom will result all summer and fall.

Shrubs grown mostly for their ornamental fruits, such as firethorns, barberries and some of the viburnums, should be pruned with caution, and as little as possible. Otherwise the autumn display of colored berries may be reduced. Dead wood and badly placed branches should be trimmed away with greatest care. Whatever thinning out is needed to keep the plants within bounds may be done in earliest spring.

When pruning shrubs with a view to obtaining the effect of colored stems in winter, it is best to cut them close to the ground in very early spring. Young shoots are always the most attractive and are in fact the only ones which show good, strong color. The red and yellow-twigged dogwoods are in this group.

There is some difference of opinion about pruning back foliage to offset loss of roots when transplanting. My experience has been that it is desirable to cut back newly transplanted shrubs quite sharply. While not as showy the first year, they will grow bushier and will develop better the second year. Another kind of pruning known as renewal or rejuvenation is applicable to the so-called "die-back" shrubs, those whose tops freeze back in winter. This group includes some of the tamarix species, certain buddleias, *Hydrangea paniculata* and its varieties (usually), *Callicarpa dichotoma* and others. When these are pruned to ground level, they make new growth readily and the rejuvenation process amounts practically to growth of a new bush. This is also the best way to handle overgrown and unsightly specimens of lilac, mock orange, forsythia and snowballs. If cut back to the soil, fertilized and thoroughly watered, these older bushes will, in most cases, produce strong new growth in due course and will bloom freely.

Pruning tools should always be sharp, so cuts are clean and not jagged. Much damage may be done with dull pruners, thoughtlessly used. To make a close clean cut, avoiding bark injury, shears should be held with the blade next to the portion of branch or twig which is to remain on the plant. A pair of well-made pruning shears, a small curved saw designed for pruning and a pair of long-handled

Mature canes of the forsythia should be cut off at ground level to rejuvenate the shrub.

Gottscho-Schleisner

lopping shears are ample for nearly all kinds of pruning, except perhaps rejuvenation of old neglected shrubs. For these a carpenter's saw
may be needed.

4

Early-flowering Shrubs

CLARENCE E. LEWIS

THE early-flowering shrubs proclaim spring's arrival on the winter
landscape. Flowering dates are not rigid but usually the first to bloom
after January 1 are the witch hazels.

The common kind (*Hamamelis virginiana*) produces blooms
during October and November, but the Chinese and vernal witch
hazels (*H. mollis* and *H. vernalis*) may flower as early as February.
The Japanese witch hazel (*H. japonica*) usually is about a week or
ten days later. All three have a pleasing fragrance, but the vernal is
the most pungent.

Flower buds, which appear on short, curved stems, vary in the
Chinese, vernal and Japanese witch hazels. The flower buds of the
Japanese witch hazel usually are in twos, pointed and brown; the
vernal and Chinese types generally are in threes, round, and yellow
to light tan. The Chinese witch hazel has extremely hairy flower
buds that are about twice the size of the vernal flower buds. Young
stems of the vernal are much duller than those of the Chinese or
Japanese kinds. Spidery petals of the vernal flowers are more orange
than yellow, while the Japanese and Chinese witch hazels have yellow
blooms.

The Cornelian cherry (*Cornus mas*) is one of our best early-
flowering shrubs, producing blooms in late March some years, but
more often in early April. The flower buds differ from those of the
flowering dogwood (*C. florida*) in that they are tan and obovately
round, while those of the native flowering dogwood are gray and

Flowering quince blossoms appear early in spring when the weather settles.

J. Horace McFarland

Ribbonlike flowers of Japanese witch hazel appear from early January into March.

J. Horace McFarland

Sunny blossoms of the aromatic spicebush are among the first to appear in spring.

J. Horace McFarland

Cornelian cherry, a member of the dogwood family, can be trained to tree form.

J. Horace McFarland

much flatter. The Cornelian cherry's yellow flowers do not have the conspicuous bracts of flowering dogwood. Cuttings of Cornelian cherry can be forced into bloom indoors during the winter.

In early or mid-April the lesser-known winter hazels (*corylopsis*) show light yellow hanging flower racemes. These large shrubs eventually produce clean, blue-green, heart-shaped leaves that appear after the flowers. Winter hazels are available, but not readily obtained from the nursery. The hardiest include the fragrant winter hazel (*C. glabrescens*), the spiked winter hazel (*C. spicata*) and the Chinese winter hazel (*C. sinensis*). The winter flower buds are semi-round, red-toned and often have loose flower bud scales. These shrubs are reluctant to grow where temperatures dip to five or ten degrees below zero, but they can be tried in a warm, sheltered site.

Seldom planted, although worthy, is the native spicebush (*Lindera benzoin*). It abounds in moist woodlands. The clusters of small, yellow, buttonlike flowers appear from early to mid-April on curved, spicily fragrant stems. The large leaves turn a clear yellow color in fall.

Not all of the early-flowering shrubs have yellow flowers. Among the broadleaved evergreen kinds, there are the white-flowered American and Japanese andromeda (*Pieris floribunda* and *P. japonica*). They bear clusters of white flowers in early April. If the temperature does not suddenly rise to the 70's, the flowers may persist for three or four weeks.

The smaller shrub (*P. floribunda*) has erect flower clusters, while the larger, colorful Japanese species has more prolific, pendant blooms. The leaves of the latter are much glossier; there often is a bronze-red winter color in the flower clusters and sometimes in the foliage. (Leaves of the American andromeda are green only.) As in all other spring-flowering species, the flower buds were formed the previous summer.

The first forsythia, Korean forsythia, precedes the other species by about a week, appearing in late March or early April. The yellow flowers are not as abundant as those of the varieties Lynwood Gold, Spring Glory or Spectabilis. But the Korean forsythia (*Forsythia ovata*) is more erect and less competitive when used with other shrubs.

Also proclaiming the spring season are early-flowering shrubs such as spring heath, pussy willow, fragrant viburnum, common flowering quince, February daphne and fragrant honeysuckle. Shrubs that flower in early spring often are affected by severe frosts. Sometimes the low temperatures are destructive enough to ruin both the flowers and the potential fruits.

Many early-flowering shrubs are excellent for espaliering. When trained against a warm south wall, they usually will bloom earlier than when in shrub form. Species that adapt to espaliering include any of the forsythias, fragrant viburnum, the winter hazels, fragrant honeysuckle, fothergilla, flowering quince and witch hazels.

Plants that are thought of as early spring-flowering shrubs need not always remain as shrubs. Some can be trained to a single standard. Examples of this are Cornelian cherry, the Japanese and vernal witch hazels, Persian parrotia, winter hazels, fothergilla and fragrant viburnum.

5

Aromatic Shrubs, Herbs and Flowers

BARBARA M. CAPEN

A SWEET fragrance wafted on a summer breeze is so delightful, it is surprising how few gardeners plan for it for their own garden. They may enjoy the perfume of honeysuckle in a weedy woodlot or lilies of the valley naturalized on an old estate, but they forget that the extra dimension of scent can be added to any small terrace or porch garden.

Herbs might well form the nucleus of any aromatic planting. Both foliage and flowers can provide fragrance. With some plants fragrance is picked up by a passing breeze; with others leaves must be crushed first.

A bed three to four feet wide and ten to fifteen feet long is large enough for a summer full of fragrance. At the back of the bed two or three plants of southernwood (*Artemisia abrotanum*), two to three feet high and wide, will form a mass of finely cut, spicy gray-green foliage. Also at the back of the bed the beebalms—*Monarda didyma* with dark red flowers and *M. fistulosa* with lavender flowers—will provide both color and fragrant foliage.

In the middle of the bed several plants of English lavender (*La-*

vandula vera) will form mounds of interesting gray foliage as well as the familiar lavender flowers. After flowers have faded, the foliage echoes their scent. Also in the middle of the bed a few plants of lemon balm (*Melissa officinalis*) will add a lemon-oil scent. Flowers are white and insignificant but the foliage is pleasant when crushed.

Either of the spicy santolinas, the gray *Santolina chamaecyparissus* or the green *S. virens*, makes an interesting edging. Both of these small plants, like lavender, are small evergreen shrubs. In severe winters the santolinas die back to the ground and grow back from the roots in summer. Along with the santolinas the common thyme (*Thymus vulgaris*) makes a foot-high edging of fine, dark green foliage. Though its fragrance, too, is airborne, it is far stronger when leaves are crushed.

In addition to these hardy herbs there are some less well-known tender ones which can be treated like annuals in colder climates, or they can be potted before frost and taken into the house for the winter. One of the most delightful is the pineapple sage (*Salvia rutilans*), which is not hardy north of Virginia. It grows into a tall shrub during the summer and late in the season produces delicate, red flowers about the same shade as the common red salvia. The rose-scented sage (*S. dorisi*) is even taller and coarser but it, too, has a delightful fragrance. Anyone who brushes against the plant with hand or clothes will be surprised at the strong perfume in the air.

There are several fragrant-leaved geraniums that are worth planting. The rose geranium is probably the best known. Several lemon-scented kinds are available, one with a large, finely cut leaf called Skeletonleaf, and Prince Rupert, with small leaves. Another pleasant addition to the group is the velvety peppermint geranium.

All of these with the exception of Prince Rupert grow to be tall and spreading plants. They are perhaps best placed as underplanting for medium-sized shrubs rather than in a bed with more delicate-growing herbs. Usually geraniums are left in pots and pushed into the soil. Before setting out the plant, place gravel in the bottom of the hole to prevent a long root from attaching itself to the earth.

Lemon verbena is another popular fragrant herb. Since it grows tall and shrubby, it could go at the back of the bed near the beebalms. Rosemary, planted just in back of the edging, is not generally hardy. It may survive two or three winters in a protected place if the weather is mild but, if possible, it should be lifted and taken into the house for the winter. Where it is hardy it will produce light blue flowers early in summer, but it is worth growing for the pungent leaves alone.

The old-fashioned four-o'clock, with its faint lemon fragrance, is a terrace favorite. It tolerates semi-shade while another old-time flower, mignonette, does better in hot sun. The delicious sweetness of violets is unforgettable and gardeners use them for their intrinsic beauty as well.

A few regal and auratum lilies planted at the back of the bed and tuberoses near the front will provide additional fragrance during the summer. If *Daphne odora* is hardy, it is worth growing for the heavy perfume of the flowers in early spring. *D. cneorum*, which is hardier though sometimes temperamental, is also worth growing for its spring perfume. The fragrant viburnums, *Viburnum carlesi* and *V. burkwoodi*, could be planted in the corner of the bed for the fragrance of their flowers in May.

In a slightly moist place the swamp azalea will thrive and surprise everyone with its unusual cinnamon-scented flowers in July. *Clethra alnifolia*, the summersweet, also likes some moisture in the soil but it will grow under drier conditions than the azalea. Summersweet produces fragrant flowers in late July and early August.

The fragrant-foliaged shrubs are few compared to the perennials, but there are two worth growing. The young foliage of the sweetbrier rose (*Rosa eglanteria*) is as fragrant as any rose. The chaste tree (*Vitex agnus-castus*) has aromatic gray-green foliage. It produces spikes of lavender flowers in August that have the same fragrance as the foliage.

6

Trees and Shrubs
for Summer Bloom

MAURICE BROOKS

So MANY trees and shrubs bloom in spring that midsummer and autumn may seem like the famine after a feast. Nevertheless, it is possible to maintain a succession of blossoms on woody plants from July until frost.

There are many handsome and dependable species. For example, the butterfly bush (*buddleia*) attracts hordes of colorful butterflies to its flowers. Blossoms range in shade from pure white, through a variety of blues and purples, to crimson. Severe winters may kill the plant to the ground, but new shoots which develop from the roots begin to flower in July. Bloom will continue until heavy frost.

Sourwood (*Oxydendrum arboreum*), another member of the heath family, produces a wealth of clustered, bell-shaped white flowers in late July. The leaves turn brilliant scarlet by early fall. Under forest conditions this plant sometimes grows to tree size; in the open it usually assumes a shrubby growth habit.

Sourwood has given its name to a Kentucky mountain as well as to a famous American square-dance tune. In addition, sourwood honey is a local specialty in the southern Appalachians.

Hydrangeas include several useful species for summer and fall bloom. Brilliant blue and pink varieties are excellent for sandy, seaside locations. *Hydrangea paniculata grandiflora* is a hardy, spreading shrub. The large heads of white flowers develop in August; the blooms turn pink as cooler weather arrives. At this stage the flowers are good material for dried arrangements.

The handsome oakleaf hydrangea (*H. quercifolia*), a native of the Southern states, has proved hardy to the vicinity of New York and Long Island. When grown farther north, the tops often die down and there is sparse flowering. This hydrangea is low growing with attractive foliage. The heads of snowy white flowers open in July.

A versatile, low-growing shrub is *Abelia grandiflora*, a member of the honeysuckle family. This semi-evergreen plant is closely allied to *linnaea*, the northern twinflower, which was Linnaeus's favorite. Pink blossoms appear on abelia in late June and persist until cold weather.

Shoots may winterkill, but sprouts from the roots will bear flowers the following summer. Abelia grows best in well-drained, acid soils which have been enriched with peat moss or leafmold.

Rose of Sharon or the althaeas are shrubby members of the mallow family. They produce large, showy blossoms. Under favorable conditions althaeas sometimes assume tree forms. The plants begin to bloom in July and they have a long flowering season.

One of America's most historic and romantic plants is franklinia (*Gordonia altamaha*), a small tree discovered more than one hundred years ago along the Altamaha River in Georgia. The tree has never been rediscovered in the wild. Nevertheless, it was preserved in Bartram's Garden near Philadelphia, Pennsylvania, and has been propagated widely.

Franklinia is a fine ornamental tree, opening large creamy white flowers in August. Blossoms remain until freezing weather. It does best in rich, sandy loam. The tree has proved hardy as far north as Boston, Massachusetts.

Blue is an unusual flower color for summer shrubs, but the chaste-tree (*Vitex agnus-castus*) bears blossoms in a variety of blue shades. It is a semi-hardy plant. Root sprouts bear flowers during the first summer of growth, although these may not appear until August or September. The blossoms rival those of buddleia in their attraction of butterflies. The chaste-tree thrives in full sunlight and fertile soil.

On the margin of dependability for northern gardens are two showy favorites of the South—crape myrtle (*Lagerstroemia indica*) and silk tree (*Albizzia julibrissin*). Both of these are exceptionally handsome summer-blooming plants.

Crape myrtle and silk tree generally succeed as far north as southern New Jersey. Both will survive farther north in sheltered coastal areas. Occasionally, severe winters may kill them. The hardier silk tree variety *rosea* thrives northward to the Boston, Massachusetts, area.

7

Guide to the Needled Evergreens

CLARENCE E. LEWIS

Among the needled evergreens are some of the finest ornamentals for landscape use. To pinpoint those plants with the best decorative qualities and good growing habits, Clarence E. Lewis has selected six major groups. In each he mentions those species and varieties of particular value. Line drawings by Peter K. Nelson show the representative characteristics of each group.

Spruce and Fir

THE firs (*Abies*) and spruces (*Picea*) are not considered the best of the narrow-leaved evergreens for the small home grounds because of their ultimate large size. This does not rule them out for larger areas where they are used for screening or as specimens. Home gardeners can choose some of the slow-growing variations. The dwarf forms of spruce can be effectively used in foundation plantings.

Both genera prefer clean air, not the heat and smoke of most cities. They also need room to spread laterally and vertically. Good soil drainage is important for their best appearance. When preparing the soil, incorporate at least one part peat moss to each part of soil.

Pruning can be done to a certain extent to shape a tree, but a branch should be removed so that no stub is left. Another way to keep such evergreens dense is by pinching out the end buds just before growth begins in spring. Pruning can be done at the same time, but it is not an operation for an untrained person.

The white fir (*Abies concolor*) is the most adaptable of the firs for a wide range of growing conditions. It has excellent blue variations that exceed the qualities of some of the blue Colorado spruces.

Firs that have a rich green foliage include Nordmann (*A. nordmanniana*), Veitch (*A. veitchi*) and Nikko fir (*A. homolepis*), which are easily obtainable. The Douglas fir (*Pseudotsuga*), not truly a fir, is well suited to ornamental Eastern and Midwestern plantings, and some good blue kinds are available.

Spruces, other than blue forms or Colorado spruce, include the excellent rich green Oriental spruce (*Picea orientalis*), the widely distributed and adaptable Norway spruce (*P. abies*), the narrow-headed Serbian spruce (*P. omorika*) and the white spruce (*P. glauca*) for the Northern states.

There are several dwarf forms of white spruce that are extremely dense and do not exceed a height of ten feet, even after many years. Included are Alberta spruce and Black Hills spruce.

The best dwarf forms of spruce are variations of the Norway spruce. They include such odd shapes as a creeping one (*P. abies procumbens*), a pendulous one (*P. abies pendula*), the dense short needled, broad-looking nest spruce (*P. abies nidiformis*) and the moundlike Gregory spruce (*P. abies gregoryana*), which is handsome.

False Cypress and Thuja

THE false cypress or retinospora (*Chamaecyparis*) and arborvitae (*Thuja*) are thought of as being similar because so many species of each have scalelike leaves. Both groups have good fibrous root systems, which encourage successful transplanting, and they can be grown in moderate shade to full sun. Moist—not wet—soils offer no serious problem, and good soil drainage plus a liberal amount of organic matter (peat moss) at planting time are recommended.

Shearing (not pruning) should be done during March and April, before growth starts. Sometimes it may be necessary to repeat this in July or August. A common occurrence in both arborvitae and false cypress is the browning and dying of inner branches and leaves during the summer and early fall. This happens after the outer new branches and leaves have developed, and it is perfectly natural.

For hedges under four feet, Globe, Woodward and Hovey arborvitaes are suitable, as are dwarf Hinoki, compact Hinoki and dwarf plume false cypress. The following make good screens or tall hedges (six to ten feet): Hinoki and plume false cypress, and Ware, wintergreen and Rosenthal arborvitae.

Taller-growing plants that can be kept in bounds are the narrow steel blue Scarab false cypress (*Chamaecyparis lawsoniana allumi*); the rich green foliaged Hinoki false cypress (*C. obtusa*) and variations of it, the fine-textured plume false cypress (*C. pisifera plumosa*), the stringlike thread false cypress (*C. pisifera filifera*) and the broad, dense but tall-growing Ware arborvitae (*Thuja occidentalis wareana*). The last may be listed as Siberian arborvitae and scientifically also as *Thuja occidentalis sibirica* or *robusta*.

Other tall-growing arborvitaes include the narrow, dense but dark green wintergreen arborvitae (*Thuja occidentalis nigra*). Rosenthal is narrow but spirally branched, as in the Douglas arborvitae.

There are several yellow, golden, gray, blue-toned and sulfur-foliaged examples of arborvitae and false cypress, but it is difficult to combine them with other plants. Also available are globe, oval and other shapes which look attractive at the nursery but do not blend well in the landscape.

As a group, the false cypress are not bothered by insects or disease. However, arborvitaes sometimes are subject to attack by red spider.

Hemlock

MANY gardeners think of hemlocks (*Tsuga*) as forest trees of great heights, but they have found a useful and respected place in the landscape of the American home. There are principally four species found in nurseries—the Canadian or eastern hemlock (*Tsuga canadensis*), the Carolina hemlock (*T. caroliniana*), the Japanese hem-

Eastern Hemlock
(*Tsuga canadensis*)

Japanese yew (*Taxus cuspidata*)

Sawara false cypress
(*Chamaecyparis pisifera*)

Common juniper
(*Juniperus communis*)

Colorado spruce (*Picea pungens*)

Japanese black pine
(*Pinus thunbergi*)

lock (*T. diversifolia*) and the Siebold hemlock (*T. sieboldi*). They are all different in appearance. The Canadian is the most widely grown and used, while the Siebold hemlock is not available in many nurseries.

The Carolina hemlock has a darker green color than the Canadian and it has a more irregular arrangement of branches and leaves. There is a tendency for the Japanese hemlock to grow as a large shrub with several main stems.

All three popular hemlocks make excellent fine-textured hedges that can be kept to a height of four to ten feet, and more if desired. It is necessary to prune them at least once a year, more often if needed. Timing is late winter or early spring, then again in July.

There are several variations of Canadian hemlock. The weeping hemlock (*T. canadensis pendula*) is best known. It is broad and spreading, with tumbling branches that look from a distance like a green waterfall. It may be, and often is, no taller than six to ten feet, but may have a canopied spread of twelve to twenty feet. It takes many years to reach this size and is well suited for either side of the broad entrance of a large building. Younger plants can be used by a home entrance. There is a slow-growing and spreading form, Curtis Dwarf, that will take six to eight years to reach a height of two feet.

Other variations are a deep green, dense-needled, slow-growing form (*T. canadensis atrovirens*), a globe form, a prostrate one and even some with golden foliage that is brightest when the new leaves are first formed. Also, an extremely small-leaved variety can be found, among others.

Shade is no problem as long as there are no low, overhanging branches, but hemlocks should have at least a half-day's sun if they are to remain dense. They resent the interference of near-by roots.

Excellent soil drainage is necessary, and hemlocks do like a liberal amount of organic matter in the soil. Do not place hemlocks where they will receive the brunt of prevailing winds or they will burn, nor place them in "closeted" areas where air circulation is poor.

Yew

THE yews (*Taxus*) are the most widely used of the narrow-leaved evergreens for home grounds planting because of their many variations of form, rich green foliage and adaptability to shade. They are fine evergreens for hedges, foundation plantings, deep shaded banks, flat areas and many other spots in sun or shade.

The major soil requirement is good drainage. They will not survive without it. The root systems are densely fibrous, which indicates that transplanting is no problem.

The only species of yew found in the East or Midwest that is not recommended for home gardens is the native Canadian yew or ground hemlock (*Taxus canadensis*), which grows in the shade of many Northern woodlands. It burns badly in sun and does not transplant easily.

Yews that do not usually grow more than four feet tall, or that may easily be kept at this height or less, include the spreading English yew (*T. baccata repandens*). It is one of the very best, with a moundlike habit and rich green foliage. Prostrate Anglojap yew (*T. media* Prostrate) has a flat spreading appearance. Other low-growing spreaders include the prostrate Japanese yew (*T. cuspidata* Prostrate), Ward yew (*T. media wardi*), dwarf Japanese yew (*T. cuspidata nana*), cushion Japanese yew (*T. cuspidata densa*) and Hill Anglojap yew (*T. media* Hill).

For compact forms, but often rounded and generally upright branching, there are the Brown, Halloran and Vermeulen yews, all *T. media*. They will grow to a height of six feet or more unless pruned.

Taller (six feet) spreading forms include Sebian yew (*T. media* Sebian), Berryhill yew (*T. media* Berryhill) and compact Japanese yew (*T. cuspidata intermedia*). Broad, vaselike forms that will grow to a height of ten feet include some very fine yews like spreading Japanese yew (*T. cuspidata expansa*), Thayer yew (*T. cuspidata thayerae*) and Hunnewell yew (*T. media* Hunnewell).

The *T. media* species also supplies some other useful variations. Narrow but tall-growing (to ten feet) yews are ably represented by Hicks, Stoveken and Costich yews. For broad upright forms there are Hatfield, Kelsey, Cole and Andorra yews.

Yews that will reach a height of twenty feet, unless restrained, include the upright Japanese yew (*T. cuspidata capitata*), Adams yew (*T. media* Adams) and the Dovaston yew (*T. baccata dovastoni*).

Juniper

THE junipers (*Juniperus*) have a wide range of forms and sizes and are one of the most adaptable evergreens for the cold areas of the Northern states. In most cases junipers prefer sun or partial shade, but not dense shade. The soil should be well drained, but it does not require generous amounts of organic matter.

Almost all of the junipers can be pruned or even sheared if it is necessary to keep them controlled. The best time to prune is in early spring before growth starts—March 1 to April 15—although there is no objection to shearing for Christmas greens. The only objectionable time is when new growth is soft, from about May 1 to June 15.

Their uses are many, and there is a form for almost every home garden need. For slopes or banks in rich or poor soil there are Bar Harbor, Waukeegan, Andorra, Oldfield, Sargent and Japgarden, which are low and spreading. Recommended for windy areas where screening is necessary are Keteleer, Hill Dundee, Silver, Red Cedar and Canaert. Where broad, vaselike forms are needed, with an ultimate height of six to eight feet, there are Pfitzer, blue Pfitzer, Hetzi and Koster.

Low-spreading or creeping forms that do not exceed a height of one to two feet even after fifteen to twenty years are Japgarden, Sargent, Shore, Douglas and Tamarix Savin, which have green foliage. For blue foliage there is a creeping Andorra that turns purple during late summer, fall and winter. For an in-between height, two to four feet, but spreading, the compact or slow-growing forms of Pfitzer and Savin junipers are recommended.

Several kinds have been omitted, such as Irish, Swedish, Spiny Greek and Meyer. Their forms or colors or both are hard to incorporate into the home landscape.

Junipers do not make the best hedges. This is particularly true where there is little sunlight or where roots must compete with those of near-by trees. During the hot, dry summer most of them are attacked by mites, causing a loss of inner foliage that is unattractive. This can be controlled by thorough spraying with a miticide.

Hardiness is no problem with most of the junipers, since they have survived temperatures of fifteen or more degrees below zero. Some wind burning may occur, but it is not serious and the plant quickly recovers. The blue fruits are quite attractive, but are more commonly found on the taller-growing forms of Chinese and red cedar junipers.

Pine

PINES, the name some people erroneously use for all narrow-leaved evergreens, include trees primarily, although there are a few smaller species. They can be used for preventing soil erosion, and some also are well suited for screening, providing a tall hedge. Or they can be used as specimen lawn or patio trees.

They are not difficult to transplant, except for such species as pitch (*Pinus rigida*) and scrub (*P. virginiana*) pines, which grow wild in sandy and stony soils. These pines are not often used in landscape planting, however.

As long as there is good drainage, soil type is not important, although pines respond to a good supply of organic matter. Pruning is done by cutting back stems or removing the terminal buds to create density. The proper time is in late winter or early spring, before growth begins.

Browning and dying of inner leaves in the summer and early

fall happens annually and is no cause for alarm. This natural process also occurs in many other evergreens.

The most widely used shrub form is the mugo pine (*P. mugo*), of which there are variations. Some have very short needles and are slow growing and dense.

The white pine (*P. strobus*), a native tree, is one of the most adaptable. There is also a narrow-growing form called pyramidal white pine, which is satisfactory, too. The red or Norway pine (*P. resinosa*) is not well suited to the home grounds, nor is the Ponderosa species (*P. ponderosa*). The loose-growing limber pine (*P. flexilis*) resembles the white, but its twisted growth is quite different— and useful.

Where wind is a factor, the Austrian pine (*P. nigra*) has proved to be a good choice. The same can be said for Scotch pine (*P. sylvestris*), particularly the short-needled forms.

Other possible selections could include the slow-growing compact Swiss stone pine (*P. cembra*), the loose-branched and pendulous-leaved Korean pine (*P. koraiensis*), the lesser-known, slow-growing Japanese white pine (*P. parviflora*), which is useful because of its lateral branching, and possibly the short-needled but dense-looking Macedonian pine (*P. peuce*).

8

Pruning Needled Evergreens

CLARENCE E. LEWIS

PRUNING is an art, but it is a challenge to those who practice it to shape or confine plants. A great deal of common sense is involved. At the outset it is important to select a plant with the right form and size for a specific location. It will be easier to train than a mature plant that must be made to conform by drastic pruning.

Even when the proper plants are selected, there are many good reasons for pruning the narrow-leaved or needled evergreens. Among them are: 1. To remove broken branches resulting from winter damage. These breaks seldom mend naturally. 2. To keep plants restricted or shaped so that they do not outgrow their functional purpose on the landscape. 3. To remove diseased branches. 4. To confine the height and width of hedges. 5. To train special trees such as white pine to give a horizontal, tierlike effect. 6. To shape espaliered plants on walls, fences or other vertical surfaces.

For pruning purposes, there are actually two divisions of needled evergreens: those that can be pruned at any time of the year because of their unorganized method of growing, and those that require special consideration because of their regular habit of growth.

In the first division, the evergreens that have an unorganized habit of growth, are the yews (*Taxus*), junipers (*Juniperus*), plum yew (*Cephalotaxus*) and torreya (*Torreya*). The last two genera resemble the yew in appearance and can be pruned in much the same manner. Also included in this group are the hemlocks (*Tsuga*), false cypress (*Chamaecyparis*), arborvitae (*Thuja*), true cypress (*Cupressus*), podocarpus (*Podocarpus*), incense cedar (*Libocedrus*) and China fir (*Cunninghamia*).

This group can often be cut more drastically either to keep the plants within bounds or to encourage greater density. The yews can be cut back to woody stems that are two, three, four or even five years old. New branches and leaves will grow from these older stems, but cutting back to stems beyond those that are three or four years old will be a gamble if the plants do not receive proper care. When new branches and new needles appear, they are soft and subject to damage

Scotch pine with all of its end buds.   *Clarence E. Lewis*

Scotch pine with all of its end buds. *Clarence E. Lewis*

TOP LEFT: Two years' growth of Scotch pine can be cut back by removing a twig to the whorl of branches.

TOP RIGHT: Mature Scotch pine with branches growing in whorls.

RIGHT: Pruning cut on Scotch pine made two years before is healing over as it should.

Clarence E. Lewis

during prolonged dry periods. This makes regular and deep watering necessary the first year or two.

The junipers, arborvitae and false cypress can be cut almost as severely as the yews. When to cut such plants is not as much of a problem as some people think it is. About the only time of year when the pruning of yews or other genera mentioned is not recommended is during the first two or three weeks of the spring growing period. Pruning can be done at this time, but it will be a delicate job unless

TOP LEFT: Tip of Colorado spruce twig with all of its end buds.

TOP RIGHT: Tip of Colorado spruce twig with one end bud removed.

RIGHT: Tip of Colorado spruce twig with all end buds removed.

Clarence E. Lewis

the gardener has an unusually sharp knife or pruning shears. Dull knives will injure the tips, and then die back will occur and brown patterns appear. The second less favorable time is in late summer; late pruning may encourage fall growth which will not harden before early frosts.

Although evergreens with unorganized growth habits can be pruned almost any time of the year, some seasons are better than others. Christmas is a good time because then the trimmings can serve as greens for holiday decorations. The very best time, however, is just before growth begins in the spring, for the cut ends will soon be covered by new foliage. But even this season is not a "must."

In the second division, the needled evergreens that have a regular growth habit, are the pines (*Pinus*), spruces (*Picea*) and firs (*Abies*). Distinct whorls of branches are formed each year on the main trunk or on side branches that terminate each year's growth. These evergreens may be pruned or controlled so that growth becomes dense. This may be done in three ways: 1. The end buds may be pinched out. 2. The long candlelike spring growth may be cut to any desirable length in early June with a sharp knife or pruning shears. 3. A complete whorl of branches and stems may be removed back to the next whorl of branches. The latter can be done almost any time of the year.

Pine, spruce and fir may exude pitch where pruned or even where branches were removed one, two or possibly three years before. A tree-wound paint will not stop the flow of this pitch; it will dry by itself eventually.

Another genus that requires special attention is the true cedar (*Cedrus*), including the species Atlas cedar (*C. atlantica*), blue Atlas cedar (*C. atlantica glauca*), cedar of Lebanon (*C. libani*) and the deodar cedar (*C. deodora*). Because of their artistic and irregular patterns, these trees should be so cut that the branches are removed close to the next inner branch that is pointed in the direction desired. These plants should not be cut so drastically that they look like sheared poodles. Their informal pattern of artistry should be preserved. Colorado blue spruce may be pruned so that it appears as a low, spreading plant. This is done by removing the leader or main trunk and guiding any side branch that becomes a vertical into a horizontal direction. Pruning will be necessary each year and possibly more often.

9

Modern Rhododendrons

ALAN W. GOLDMAN

THE enormous rhododendrons of yesteryear, which graced the large estates reminiscent of England's sprawling manors, are being replaced with neater, scaled-down evergreen shrubs. This new class of rhodo-

Among the dwarf rhododendrons is Purple Gem, which rarely exceeds two and one-half feet in height.

Landscape by Henry M. Feil; Gottscho-Schleisner

dendrons, with growth measured in inches rather than feet, is far better suited to the smaller suburban plot.

Outstanding among modern rhododendrons is Windbeam, first raised by G. G. Nearing. It is extremely free flowering and bears pure white blossoms. Exhibiting an air of compact grace, the plant is an excellent choice in front of the foundation of a modern one-story or split-level house. Windbeam also may be used as a low, flowering hedge since the slender leaves remain in good condition throughout the fifty weeks of the year that the plant is out of bloom. Of unquestionable hardiness, it is reported to flower regularly on a windswept Connecticut hillside.

From the same breeder comes the group of semi-dwarf rhododendrons called the Guyencourt hybrids. All six varieties are similar in appearance when out of bloom—they have long, narrow, hairy evergreen leaves and a growth habit very similar to the Japanese barberry.

The Guyencourt hybrids are exceptionally good looking when planted in groups, since the individual plants tend to grow in an open fashion unless held back by tip pruning after bloom. Lenape, a very pale yellow, can be set in a group of pure white Montchanin. Brandywine, pale pink in bud, seems to combine well with Chesapeake, Delaware or Hockessin. The last three mentioned open with an apricot tint, then turn white.

For gardeners who seek scarlet flowers in a rhododendron, Kluis

Sensation should be an extremely satisfying plant. It looks more like a typical rhododendron than the dwarfs mentioned earlier. The plant is full and bushy with an erect pod of bright scarlet flowers, frilled at the edges. It will tolerate temperatures down to five degrees below zero and will bloom regularly in late May. Lower winter temperatures may damage some of the vivid blossoms.

Any listing of rhododendrons should include the Dexter hybrids. These unique hardy plants were developed by the almost legendary C. O. Dexter. Starting in 1926, Mr. Dexter raised almost 20,000 rhododendrons a year from his own crosses. The plants were unusual for two reasons—the flowers were large and decorative and the plants hardy enough to thrive in the extremely cold Northeastern winters. Unfortunately, many counterfeit Dexter hybrids have flooded the Eastern market.

It is best to get the advice of a knowledgeable rhododendron specialist before purchasing a shrub identified as a Dexter. My favorite is Parker's Pink—a soft pink when in bloom and unusually pleasant to look at with its thrifty habit and light foliage.

The Hillier Nursery in Winchester, England, introduced a compact, low-growing hybrid, Arthur J. Ivens, in the spring of 1944. This plant is just beginning to be seen in better nurseries in the East. The leaves are small and roughly heart-shaped, unusual in a hardy rhodo-

Hybrid rhododendrons provide spectacular display in June.

Gottscho-Schleisner

dendron. This hybrid variety can withstand temperatures as low as fifteen degrees below zero.

Shallow, bell-like blossoms, the color of a strawberry ice-cream soda, open in late April. After the blossoms have fallen, another show of color begins, equally striking to the eye. Arthur J. Ivens puts out new growth of a peculiar red-bronze hue. Actually, anyone fortunate enough to own this semi-dwarf evergreen plant can count on five or six weeks of color in one corner of the garden.

No list of new rhododendrons would be more than half complete without at least a quick reference to the azalea side of the family. The most satisfying azalea to be developed in many years is the low-growing hybrid Gumpo. This evergreen shrub seems to have been designed especially to grow in front of an evergreen planting of rhododendrons or low-growing conifers.

Gumpo never grows over fifteen inches high. Its generous annual growth spreads horizontally rather than vertically. In late June each terminal opens a pair of pure white flat flowers, almost three inches in diameter. Then, for at least another three weeks, there is a sporadic show of snowy white on the more shaded parts of the plant. Although Gumpo was developed by K. Wada of Japan, the azalea shows none of the tortuous growth habits so often associated with Japanese shrubs.

1 0

Pruning Rhododendrons

ALAN W. GOLDMAN

THE home owner often is reluctant to prune a rhododendron that has grown out of bounds, because the shrub represents a sizable investment—especially when it has grown to the size where drastic pruning is necessary. Yet when a large rhododendron has outgrown its location, drastic pruning is the answer. April is the best time to prune rhododendrons.

Since the shrub must be cut over completely, the owner should steel himself to the loss of flowers for one year. If only half the plant is cut back, the goal will not be achieved at all. Instead, the cut-over section will remain dormant while the growing energy will be channeled into the uncut part. The result is a plant more out of shape than before pruning.

When pruning a rhododendron, the best place to make the actual cut is just above the dormant growth bud on the old wood. The dormant growth bud is the point where, in previous summers, the shrub put on a late spurt of growth, which is called "growing through." It is a primary cause of legginess.

Under normal conditions the shrub forms a flower bud just above the dormant growth bud. Then, after the flower is spent, the dormant growth bud produces a few side shoots to make the plant thrifty and full in appearance.

However, if high temperatures and heavy rainfall occur in autumn, the flower bud turns into a leaf bud and starts into growth the same year it is formed. The dormant growth bud remains dormant and vertical growth is made by the plant at the expense of lateral growth.

Cuts should be made at 90 degrees to the twig and never more than one-half inch above a dormant bud. Wounds need not be painted but the tool used for pruning should be sharp to avoid shredding or tearing of the bark. Pruning shears are best for the operation.

Rhododendrons should not be fertilized immediately after extensive pruning since the cut-over shrub has no foliage to take the feeding. Heavy mulching should be avoided, too. After the first growth has appeared, though, a mulch of wood chips, pine needles or oak leaves should be renewed.

Two forms of minor pruning are used in rhododendron care. Deadheading is the removal of spent flower blossoms before they have had a chance to mature into seed pods. One rhododendron authority claims that forming seed pods uses up seven times more energy than forming flower buds.

On a rhododendron that has just finished blooming, new soft growth begins to push out from just below the spent bud. When deadheading, reasonable care should be exercised to avoid removal of new growth along with faded blooms, for this growth forms the future scaffolding of the shrub as well as the next year's flowers.

Small shears, a pruning knife or even the gardener's thumbnail will do the job.

Disbudding, the other form of minor pruning, is the removal of flower or leaf buds while they are still tight and undeveloped. It requires a knowledge of rhododendron blooming and growth habits.

On a very young shrub, terminal leaf buds are "taken" in spring to force the plant to develop a rounded shape. (The terminal leaf bud is thinner and more pointed than the fat, terminal flower bud.) Exceptionally good late-summer weather may force a more mature shrub to form two, three or even four flower buds at the branch terminals.

All but one of these flower buds should be taken since the plant presents an unattractive appearance if allowed to develop and flower. The blooms will be small and puny. It is far better to force a single flower bud to magnificent bloom at each apex.

From time to time a grafted rhododendron will sucker—that is, it will develop green shoots below the graft. They can be recognized by the difference in the leaf shape of the understock and grafted variety. Suckers should be chopped out with a sharp spade. Merely cutting them back will only cause them to return with renewed vigor.

1 1

Azaleas for May Color

DAVID G. LEACH

FEW shrubs grace gardens with greater distinction than the azaleas. So many new varieties have been introduced that the gardener may have a difficult time making a selection.

Of the two types of azaleas, persistent-leaved (evergreen) and those that lose their leaves (deciduous) in the fall, the persistent-leaved are the more popular wherever the climate allows their cultivation. Many landscape architects feel that they are too widely planted,

Selected varieties of azaleas and dogwood blend to brighten a Maytime landscape.

Gottscho-Schleisner

especially when the suburbs break out each spring in a harsh rash of violent color.

The introduction of the Glenn Dale hybrids by the United States Department of Agriculture twenty years ago promised relief from the standardized blobs of raw color. Most landscapers thought that the older sorts would be replaced by the government-sponsored introductions with their range of much clearer, softer and more subtle shades. But the stream of Glenn Dale novelties became a flood of almost 500 different hybrids, many of them not hardy in the North. The effort of isolating those that were both hardy and good defeated their popularity in colder climates.

In the course of the last several years some varieties have emerged from the long roster of Glenn Dale hybrids as the hardiest in this large group. Northern gardeners who seek finer color and larger flowers in persistent-leaved azaleas will welcome these newer sorts:

Sebastian, with rose hose-in-hose flowers, blooms in early April; Trouper, nopal red, mid-April; and Aphrodite, free-blooming pale rose-pink, late April. Also blooming in late April are Daphnis, Tyrian pink; Illusion, deep rose-pink, blotched, low grower; and Rosette, four-inch-wide light purple double flowers. Glacier, with three-inch-wide white flowers, and Treasure, with pale pink buds opening to white flowers, four and one-half inches across, are of phenomenal quality. In late April the shrubs form great snowbanks of massed blossoms.

Continuing the succession of bloom are these fine Glenn Dale hybrids: Nerissa, brilliant deep rose-pink, yellow overlay, early May; Gaiety, pale rose-pink, blotched rose-red, early May; Anthem, rose-pink, mid-May; Delos, floriferous double rose-pink, mid-May; and Manhattan, amaranth pink, darker blotch, late May.

It is hard to define the exact hardiness limit of these Glenn Dale azaleas. They are hardier in well-drained sandy soil than in heavy soil. Most specialists consider them to be satisfactory in southern Pennsylvania, southern New Jersey, on Long Island and along the coast well into New England. The azaleas are hardier when planted with a northern exposure, sheltered toward the south, than in an open situation. Older specimens are hardier than small young plants.

The Gable hybrids are an entirely different race of persistent-leaved azaleas, emphatically hardier than any of the Glenn Dales.

Yodogawa azalea blooms with the daffodils.   *Gottscho-Schleisner*

Here again an extensive list confronts the uninitiated, but in recent years five clones have come to be almost universally regarded as both superior and hardy: Springtime, a lively pink, probably the hardiest Gable hybrid; Louise Gable, smooth salmon-pink, semi-double; Stewartstonian, clear bright red; Rose Greeley, white; and Big Joe, lilac.

For the ultimate in hardiness, there are the azaleas developed by nurseryman Orlando Pride in the severe climate of Butler, Pennsylvania. They are not quite the equal of the Gable hybrids in quality and color range, but they can be successfully grown in regions designated as Hardiness Zone 5, a remarkable northward leap in the cultivation of persistent-leaved azaleas.

The new Pride hybrids are only sparingly available as named clones, but seedlings in pink shades are more freely sold. They bring to all but the very coldest parts of the Northeast the eye-catching drama of azalea color in springtime.

The Exbury and Knap Hill hybrids from England are still the best of the deciduous azaleas. Only the deciduous azaleas have a flower color range that includes yellow, and only they can provide the marvelous pastel range of subtle shades, the electric scarlets devoid of any trace of blue, immense flowers in coral and shrimp pink. Moreover, the blooms often are fragrant and may be ruffled and fluted as well. The English imports have elevated these attractions to an entirely new standard of excellence.

Fanciers delight in the new English hybrids for their great improvement over the coarse, short-lived Mollis hybrids that have dominated nursery lists for generations. But here again the offerings are overly large in number.

The following new English introductions rate a resounding vote of approval: Old Gold, unique deep yellow shade, flushed orange; Orange Ade, soft orange; Satan, clear, vivid scarlet; Persil, white; Toucan, cream, fading white, very large; Cecile, enormous pale pink blooms flushed deep pink; and Sunset Boulevard, luminous clear pink. Also excellent are Honeysuckle, cream, faintly brushed pink; Strawberry Ice, a distinctive shade of salmon-pink; and Princess Royal, ivory, flushed pink with yellow blotch.

Most of the Exbury and Knap Hill azaleas appear to be winter-hardy almost anywhere in the Northeastern United States. It will take a few years to determine which are best suited in flower substance and in vigor to our hot Eastern springs and summers. In the meantime, the above list provides startling innovations in flower color and form for gardeners interested in the good, the new and the different.

12

The Stately Camellias

CLAUDE CHIDAMIAN

AFTER a century of decline and neglect, camellias are making a brilliant comeback. From British Columbia to California, from Texas to Virginia—and even further north and east—gardeners are finding these choice evergreens as rugged and adaptable as their native pines and oaks.

Camellias are common forest trees or shrubs in Southeastern Asia. They grow in thin woodlands, in verdant valleys and on rugged hillsides rooted in well-drained soils enriched by continuous layers of forest mold. These camellias receive abundant rainfall and continued high humidity. While there is no wide fluctuation in the daily temperature, the plants are often covered with snow in winter and are basked in above 90-degree weather in summer.

To grow camellias successfully, gardeners must first accept them as common woodland plants and then adapt local conditions to duplicate natural requirements: partial shade, a porous soil well supplied with humus, good drainage, uniform moisture and humidity and even temperature. Wherever there is considerable heat, wind or drought in summer, camellias must be planted in a partially shaded location. Filtered sunlight under deep-rooted, high branching trees is ideal, but where such natural shade is not available, an inexpensive lath house (with lath spaced about two inches apart) will serve as well. Adequate shading is also necessary in colder areas, where the shelter of trees, buildings or lath protects camellias from ordinary frosts and provides the necessary shade for gradual thawing the morning after a severe freeze.

In coastal areas with equable temperatures and high humidity, camellias will bloom profusely in full sunlight, but they must be protected by a lath or burlap shelter the first summer. The roots are always kept cool and moist with a two or three-inch mulch of leaves.

In nature camellias thrive in a slightly acid soil that is at least 50 per cent humus—coarse mountain soil or fertile valley loam overlaid by a deep blanket of rotting leaves, twigs and blossoms. That is why half the planting soil should consist of leafmold or peat moss and a conditioner such as granulated charcoal or perlite. In sandy soils these materials improve fertility and water retention; in alkaline soils they help to maintain acidity; in heavy soils they improve texture and drainage.

Such humus soils must always be firmly packed when planting. The camellia is set an inch or two above the surrounding soil level to allow for eventual settling as these materials decay. Once properly planted, camellias need only a coarse mulch of oak leaves, pine needles or compost at their base to keep roots cool and moist, to eliminate cultivation and to add fertility to the soil. If further feeding is needed, a simple organic fertilizer such as cottonseed meal may be applied three times each season—in fall as the flower buds are enlarging, in spring before new growth begins and in early summer as growth matures.

Providing good drainage for camellias can be a problem in lowlands, over soil hardpan, or in alkaline areas. Here they are best planted in raised beds of prepared soil 18 to 24 inches deep or, better still, in pots or tubs. Not only are camellias perfectly adapted to containers, but the potted plants may be moved about the garden, porch or terrace wherever they will grow and bloom most effectively.

Once planted, camellias must be watered carefully and generously. Adequate shading and mulching will help conserve moisture, of course, but the soil should be checked regularly and watered deeply— but not too frequently. Frequent shallow waterings are dangerous because they do not aerate the soil and because they develop a superficial root system which is quickly killed by drought. Constant humidity in the air is equally important to camellias. Spraying them overhead with a fine mist of water early in the morning or evening will keep the foliage free of dust and control pests.

Of the more than eighty species of camellia known, only four are common in American gardens and greenhouses. The first and most important is *Camellia japonica,* the finest shrub for specimen, border and foundation plantings and the perfect flower for arrangements and corsages. With more than 3,000 varieties to choose from, *japonica* offers a wonderful range of forms and foliage, colors and season, beginning in September and ending in May. Blossoms may be single, semi-double, double, anemone or peoniform; white, pink, red or variegated. Flowers range from miniatures, two inches in diameter, to show blooms over six. A basic collection should include the semi-double red Adolphe Audusson, double white Alba Plena, red and white peoniform Daikagura, pale pink peoniform Debutante, red and white semi-double Donckelari, pink and white anemoniform Elegans (Chandler) variegated, semi-double white Finlandia, red and white peoniform Gigantea, double red Glen 40, pink and white semi-double Magnoliaeflora and the red semi-double Mathotiana.

While some varieties of *Camellia japonica*—such as Berenice Boddy, Flame, Kumasaka, Tricolor—might survive zero-degree weather without special protection, both plant and flower buds of most *japonicas* would be damaged.

The truly hardy camellia has not yet been developed, but there is hope in a group of hybrids of *C. japonica* and *C. saluenensis* known collectively as the Williamsi hybrids. They have found great favor because they seem hardier than either parent, because they produce a profusion of attractive three or four-inch flowers from midseason to late. These hybrids are primarily landscape plants, and varieties such as the pale pink single J. C. Williams, deep pink semi-double Donation or silvery pink Citation will make a wonderful show in any border or foundation planting.

The flowers of *C. sasanqua* are so fragile they can seldom be cut; the young growth is so lanky, it seems vinelike. The plant is more tender than most, yet it is the most versatile of all camellias. *C. sasanqua* is a more beautiful hedge than privet, is more interesting for espalier than the roses and is a brighter and more lasting groundcover than ivy. This camellia is elegant as a hanging basket and dainty as a dwarf potted tree, the Japanese bonsai. It is the earliest camellia, blooming in fall and winter with generally smaller leaves and flowers than *C. japonica* or its hybrids. For a start some of the outstanding varieties are crimson single Hinode-no-umi, pale pink double Jean May, picoteed white and red Ocean Springs, semi-double Setsugekka, pale pink single Shinonome or the pink and white Yae-arare.

Last but certainly not least is the Queen of the clan, *C. reticulata*. Silky, iridescent blooms come midseaon and late, and frequently exceed eight inches in diameter. The flowers are usually borne on plants so lanky, so sparse-leaved, so treelike that they are of relatively little value in landscaping. Worse still, this species is tender and, except in the most favored areas, it must usually be grown under glass. But despite these faults, the wondrous blooms are the prize of every collector. Whether one chooses the amazing semi-double rose Buddha, ruffled pink Butterfly Wings, rich Crimson Robe, red and white peoniform Lionhead, deep red semi-double Noble Pearl or the orchid pink Willow Wand, each is a masterpiece of floral perfection.

1 3

Camellias for Yankees

MARJORIE SAMPLE

ENTHUSIASM is high among those who are growing camellias north of the traditional camellia belt. As more facts are gathered each year, gardeners are learning how it can be done.

Camellias were first brought to the New York area around 1800. They were then considered handsome plants to grow in conservatories and greenhouses, not garden plants. Their popularity waned, however, and the chrysanthemums became front runners.

Perhaps it was not until 1928, when the late Dr. P. W. Zimmerman planted a *Camellia japonica* outdoors in his Yonkers, New York, garden, that anyone recognized the possibility of growing these plants in the North. That particular camellia survived the winter of 1933-34 when the temperature dropped to —20 degrees. Unfortunately, the label was lost, and as yet the variety has not been identified.

Other camellias were planted; they survived temperatures of zero to —7 degrees. In 1955 Dr. Zimmerman gave good hardiness ratings to a number of camellias, among them the pink varieties Kumasaka and Lady Clare, variegated Elegans (Chandler), red-flowered Blood of China and a white variety, Purity.

All of these types now are growing in various locations near New York City. In fact, camellias now are growing in gardens in Virginia, Washington, D. C., Maryland, Pennsylvania, New Jersey, Rhode Island and Long Island.

There are many camellia species in the clan, and breeding work is being done, but these will be the hardy camellias of the future. At present, both the old and newer varieties of *Camellia japonica* are growing north of the Mason-Dixon Line.

All camellia colors are included in these *japonica* varieties. Varieties with pink and red blooms predominate. Among the pink semi-doubles are Christine Lee, Bernice Boddy, Rev. John G. Drayton, Magnoliaflora and Gloire de Nantes. The reds include single-flowered Kimberley and rose-flowered doubles Mathotiana, Glenn 40, Monjisu and Governor Mouton. Tricolor (Siebold), a semi-double, white-streaked carmine, has been successful, as has Triphosa, a semi-double white. One specimen of Yohei-haku (September Morn), with semi-double white flowers, has bloomed in April rather than in the fall, as it does in the South. It is growing in a well-protected and shaded position.

In their native lands of the Far East, camellias are found in the woods and forests where rainfall is frequent and the soil porous but capable of holding moisture. For success in growing them outdoors, these conditions should be duplicated as nearly as possible. Early spring is the recommended planting time.

Tests have shown that camellias can be grown in a wide range of soil pH (degree of acidity), but their preference seems to be for slightly acid soil. Organic material is of importance for its moisture-holding capacity and its food value to the plant. Humus, or a combination of humus and peat, should be added generously to sandy loam to form a soil mixture suitable for growth. This mixture should be in ample quantity for each plant. Good drainage is essential and the plants should never lack soil moisture.

Careful thought should be given to the selection of the planting site. Camellias are long-lived, and in the South, there are plants over 100 years old which have attained heights of twenty feet or more. In the short period of observing northern plants, the rate of growth has been surprising. Two-foot camellias have doubled in size in three to four years, and in five to six years they have shown the necessity of providing sufficient space for growth. Once established, it is unwise to move a camellia and a little forethought will save later problems.

Selected hardy varieties of camellias will endure moderate northern winters if they are provided with a sheltered site or a windbreak.

Gottscho-Schleisner

The site selected should be partly shaded and sheltered. The filtered sun under high pines is suitable, but not always available. The shade of deep-rooted deciduous or evergreen trees, separately or in combination, or the shade from buildings, walls or hedges, often will be adequate for summer and provide the necessary winter protection. A northern exposure is excellent if there is a windbreak. Sunburned leaves and damaged or blasted flower buds have resulted when plants were not shaded in winter from the bright sun in eastern and southern exposures.

If there is no naturally sheltered location available, a temporary winter windbreak may be used until trees and shrubs can be grown to provide protection. Even in the best situations, many growers protect plants for the first two or three winters until they are established, usually with a burlap-covered frame similar to that used for boxwood.

When selecting camellia plants, look for those that are well branched and sturdy with many leaf buds. Older plants are easier to establish. When actually planting, place the top of the roots well above the surrounding soil level and mulch them with an organic material. Pine needles are excellent, as are oak and beech leaves or rough humus or compost.

When properly planted, camellias require a minimum of care. As landscaping plants they are fine assets with their broad leaves and spring flowers.

1 4

The Best of the Hollies

HARRY W. DENGLER

THE holly family, which includes the genus *Ilex*, contains some of the oldest trees and shrubs cultivated by man. The Greeks grew the English holly, *Ilex aquifolium*, before the Roman Empire was established, while the Chinese used the berried branches of *I. chinensis*, the ev-

An interesting texture pattern of evergreen foliage is formed by contrasting Japanese holly, pyracantha and azaleas. Pachysandra forms a leafy border.

Landscape by William A. Rutherford; Gottscho-Schleisner

erlasting red, for New Year decorations since time immemorial. There are over 500 species scattered throughout the world, including trees and shrubs which are evergreen or deciduous, spiny-leaved or spineless with red, orange, yellow, black and, in a few instances, white colored fruits.

As the popularity of the hollies steadily increases and their landscape values are appreciated, more and more novelties or plants for specific purposes are being discovered and named. This presents a bewildering puzzle to homeowners who want to select the best species for planting. Their only recourse is a visit to a nearby arboretum, consultation with a reliable nurseryman or conference with a holly hobbyist. One fact, however, must be remembered: hollies are dioecious; generally only female plants produce fruits while male plants of the same species must be included in the planting or be nearby to insure the proper setting of berries.

Among the many species readily available from nurserymen, none are more popular, more hardy or useful for a wide range of landscape purposes than the Japanese holly. Botanically named *I. crenata*— sometimes called the black holly because of the ebony color of its fruits —this plant is in no way as spectacular as its taller-growing, red-fruited and spiny-leaved American and English holly relatives.

Native throughout all the islands of Japan, *I. crenata* is a compact, broadleaved evergreen shrub, two to five feet high, but it may grow to a height of twenty feet. The leaves are a shiny dark green, obovate in outline, from one-half to one inch long by one-quarter to one-half inch wide. The flowers of both sexes are small, yellow-white in color, generally borne in profusion and of little ornamental value. The fruit is jet black and not overly conspicuous.

There are over 75 named varieties of Japanese holly, including types suitable for formal or informal hedges of varying heights, for barriers, screens, specimens, accent plants, foundation plantings, edgings for flower borders, walks or drives, groundcovers, espaliers, topiary, bonsai, backgrounds for flower beds, Japanese gardens, outdoor planters, and for streets, patios or foyers when planted in attractive containers. Heavily fruited females may appear chlorotic in winter and for this reason many landscape gardeners prefer male varieties.

The variety *convexa* has cup-shaped leaves and is an acceptable substitute for box in climates not more vigorous than Boston's. *Helleri*, Green Pygmy, Kingsville and Kingsville Green Cushion are low-growing, dwarf types. *Latifolia* is a rather vigorous grower—it often attains a height of twenty feet—with larger leaves and is suitable for high hedges and screens. Oconee River, buxifolia and Highlander are upright-growing or columnar types and useful for tall, narrow hedges.

Japanese hollies are winter hardy in areas where temperatures do not generally go below zero, but lower-growing forms have survived much severer weather when covered with an insulating blanket of snow. Highlander is said to have been undamaged at —20 degrees in West Virginia.

Yunnan holly (*I. yunnanensis*) from western China, is an evergreen shrub, five to twelve feet high. It somewhat resembles the Japanese holly, but has the advantage of bearing red fruit. It is hardy as far north as Boston. Male plants have been observed bearing fairly abundant crops of fruit approximately one third the size of female berries.

Hardiest of all North American hollies is the Winterberry (*I. verticillata*), a deciduous shrub or small tree that grows to a height of twenty feet, which may be found from Nova Scotia to Wisconsin and southward into Florida. Also known as coonberry, Michigan holly or black alder—because the leaves turn brown or black after the first frost—this species inhabits open swamps and low woodlands but will tolerate much drier soils. The fruit is a bright, glossy red, borne singly or in clusters of two's and three's and colors early in the fall. Berried branches—stripped of their leaves if necessary—combine most effectively with laurel, rhododendron and most evergreens to form handsome autumn, Thanksgiving, and Christmas arrangements.

Closely related to *I. verticillata* is the smooth winterberry, a deciduous shrub that grows to ten feet high and is native to the lowland areas from Maine southward. The fruit of this species, *I. laevigata,* is borne singly, is commonly orange-red and is retained on the plants longer than that of the common winterberry. While slightly less hardy than *verticillata,* its smaller habit and the fact that the leaves turn an attractive yellow with first frost, makes the smooth winterberry somewhat more generally useful for landscape purposes. This is one of the more handsome, northern native shrubs and much more deserving of wider planting.

From Washington, D. C., westward into Oklahoma, and southward, the possumhaw holly (*I. decidua*) has few equals among the deciduous, red-berried plants of North America. This superb holly has bright orange to red fruits which persist into late spring and present a bold and gay sight throughout the winter months. It forms a large shrub or small tree that grows to a height of twenty-five feet and is a desirable small shade tree for one-story houses throughout the South.

Another good deciduous, red-berried type is the fine-toothed holly (*I. serrata*) of China and Japan. It closely resembles the native winterberry except that the plant grows only six feet high and has smaller leaves and fruit. Berries are borne in abundance and are among the earliest of all hollies to color in early fall. Specimens have survived at —15 degrees in Michigan.

Most thoughts of holly, of course, center around those two most commonly associated with the Christmas season: native American holly (*I. opaca*) and its colorful English cousin from Europe (*I. aquifolium*). There are over 100 selections of the American holly, including yellow-fruiting kinds and some northern varieties hardy to —10 degrees. Distinctive here are Maryland Dwarf and Pin Cushion; both have full-sized, spiny evergreen leaves and red berries but they are dwarf in habit, permitting their use where low-growing plants are necessary. Less hardy but superb when well grown are the many English forms

Ilex cornuta.   Walter Singer

Ilex aquifolium.   Roche

Ilex opaca.   Walter Singer

Ilex verticillata.   Roche

now available. Strikingly unusual are the gold and silver variegated-leaved and pendulous types. The petite-leaved *angustifolia* is a handsome accent or specimen plant in the small garden. In the South the yaupon (*I. vomitoria*) is an attractive, small evergreen tree. Yellow-fruiting, dwarf, pendulous and variegated-leaved types are now on the market.

Other hollies of landscape value include *I. pernyi,* a red-berried type with small spiny leaves; it is hardier than commonly believed. Completely different is the long-stalked holly (*I. pendunculosa*) with spineless leaves that resemble laurel and with red fruit on drooping stems up to two inches long—this is considered one of the hardiest of the evergreen hollies. Southward of New Jersey the horned or Chinese holly (*I. cornuta*) is an exotic-appearing and popular plant. Over 70 varieties have been named—many of the females produce fruit without pollen from male plants.

A dwarf type is little known and excellent for such places where low plants are desirable. Attractively tubbed, it makes a superb patio or roof garden plant where it can be given indoor protection during winter in the North or some shade and water as needed in the hotter, drier sections of the United States.

1 5

Transplanting Evergreens

ALAN W. GOLDMAN

EVERGREENS can be moved successfully in spring or early fall, if given reasonable care and if preparation is made beforehand.

Transplanting begins with careful preparation of the new site. The area should have good air and water drainage. A hillside is excellent for air drainage and frost protection. A low pocket of ground is not. Large soil particles (sandy loam) drain well, while soils of small-size particles (clays) drain slowly and should be avoided. Evergreens like water, but not excessive amounts.

Dig a hole about 50 per cent larger than the root ball of the evergreen. If the site is close to the house or if the house was built only recently, pay special attention to routing out chunks of mortar or debris that the builder may have buried just below the surface. Building mortar is high in lime and will depress the acidity of the soil. If the soil is not naturally acid, scatter a handful of powdered sulfur on the surface of the ground when transplanting is completed. Sulfur will increase the acidity.

If a four-foot-high evergreen is to be moved, the new hole should be about two feet deep. It is a good idea to loosen the soil at the bottom of the hole to aid drainage and to insure that roots will "grow out" into the surrounding area. This expansion of the root system is a sure way to help a plant establish itself quickly.

Liberal quantities of peat moss should be incorporated into the loosened soil at the bottom of the hole—a half-bushel or more of peat moss. It should be moist, a natural condition if the bale is stored outdoors. Indoor-stored bales can be moistened by poking a hole in the top of the bale with a crowbar, and letting a trickle of water from the garden hose run into it.

Newly purchased evergreens from the nursery are sold balled and burlapped (B & B), ready for transplanting. These plants are set in the prepared planting hole at the same depth they grew in the nursery.

If an established evergreen is to be moved from one part of the garden to another, the old plant must be dug out with utmost care. Tie the pendulous branches of the shrub together with strips of cloth or soft butcher's twine. Remove whatever mulch may be on the ground around it. Measure out the root ball by this rule of thumb: For every foot of shrub diameter, measure out three inches from the main trunk of the evergreen. A rhododendron with a three-foot branch spread will have a root ball with a radius of about nine inches. Trace a circle on the ground approximating the root ball's size.

Next, with a trowel or small hand spade, dig away a few inches of earth all along the circumference line. Then make a shallow trench to guide the full-size spade. Slant the spade toward the shrub and cut into the soil. This gives a slope to the sides of the root ball. Continue to excavate around the root ball to the required depth. A three-foot shrub will have roots extending about a foot deep.

Rock the free plant over to the side with a short-handled spade and examine the root area. Gently reduce the size of the ball until the

TOP LEFT: Two or three spading forks may be used to lift the root ball of the rhododendron which is to be transplanted.

TOP RIGHT: A burlap wrap secures the root ball of the plant for safe transporting.

LEFT: Lift the shrub from the bottom, never by the stem, to avoid strain on the crown and root ball.

BOTTOM LEFT: Set the plant into the new planting hole and tamp the soil firmly into place.

BOTTOM RIGHT: A circular ridge of soil banked around the plant keeps the water where it belongs.

Herman Gantner

first few fine hairlike rootlets begin to show. These fine roots are white and easily seen—if they are destroyed in the transplanting, they will regrow quickly when the shrub is planted.

The easiest way to carry an evergreen with least disturbance is to use a square of burlap as a "stretcher." Never lift an evergreen by its trunk. The unsupported weight of the root ball will put a strain on the crown of the plant.

After the square of burlap has been worked under the root ball, have a helper lift two corners of the burlap while you lift the remaining two. This method eliminates tying up the burlap.

A cardinal rule to follow when relocating an evergreen is this: Never plant the shrub deeper than it grew before. More costly evergreens are lost through neglect of this simple precaution than in any other way. Use a half-and-half mixture of moistened peat moss and garden soil to build a cushion under the shrub to raise it to its proper level. Then jam more of this same mixture between the root ball and the outline of the planting hole. For a B & B evergreen, untie the burlap and let it fall around the base of the planting hole. The fabric will eventually disintegrate.

Next, tamp the soil mixture into place with your feet. The network of fine roots must be in close contact with the new soil so that the roots will expand into the surrounding area and establish the evergreen in its new location. Use a garden hose to soak the area to allow the soil to settle still further. A one or two-inch ridge of soil around the base of the evergreen is helpful in catching spring rain and preventing water run-off.

Fertilize as soon as possible after transplanting is completed in spring. In no instance should fertilizing be postponed beyond May. For fall planting, withhold fertilizer until spring. This advice often is neglected by gardeners eager to force the most growth from their plants; loss of the shrub is a common result. Late fertilizing prolongs the period of natural growth, so that the plant cannot slow down its production of foliage and wood. When cool weather comes, the plant still is growing and the new wood is soft and delicate. The first cold snap in the fall freezes the water in the cells of the new soft wood and the affected portion dies.

The old stand-by, cottonseed meal, is one of the best organic sources of nitrogen. Add one part superphosphate to four parts cottonseed meal for a more balanced mixture. The resulting yellow powder should be scattered lightly over the ground from the trunk of the shrub out to the branch tips. Use a double handful for every foot of shrub height. It is not necessary to wash this mixture off the leaves as it cannot burn. Some growers prefer to use a packaged acid fertilizer.

Never attempt to scratch the fertilizer into the ground—merely scatter it and let rain and frequent waterings wash it down to the roots. Since most of the roots of evergreens are close to the surface, raking or hoeing the ground will destroy the fine network of hairline surface feeders.

To protect the root system it is wise to apply a three-inch mulch of pine needles, wood chips, peanut hulls, oak leaves or other light, easily moistened material. Avoid using granulated peat moss as a mulch because it may become crusted in the dry summer months.

During the hot days of summer broadleaved evergreens will respond to a little extra attention each week. The foliage of broadleaved evergreens is an excellent indicator of soil moisture. When the leaves of rhododendrons, azaleas, camellias or hollies begin to droop, additional water is needed. The roots of these evergreens are extremely fine and close to the surface. Long periods of drought destroy the shallow roots and force the shrub to expend its small store of energy by producing new rootlets.

Within about three hours after a good soaking, the drooping foliage will become erect; this indicates how quickly water travels from the roots to the leaves.

1 6

Leaf Sprays Guard Evergreens

L. L. BAUMGARTNER

SOME of the greatest and most costly disappointments in gardening have come from annual winter losses and major damage to evergreen plants.

There are several kinds of winter damage. When plants are not hardy in the areas where they are planted, the fluid in the leaves freezes and breaks up the cell structure. At present there is little protection against this type of freezing.

A more common form of winter damage results when the soil freezes and lifts, or heaves. In these instances the fine feeder roots may be torn from the plant as it is pushed upward by the soil.

The most frequent and certainly the most serious form of winter damage is desiccation or sun-scald. Although plants appear to be dormant, high daytime temperatures and bright sun can cause the plants to continue high rates of metabolism. This requires large quantities of water. When the soil is frozen, limited quantities of water are available. If the supply is insufficient, leaf burning results.

This condition occurs in early winter (December) as plants are entering dormancy and again in late winter or early spring (February and March) as plants are breaking dormancy. Day length and the position of the sun are about the same for both periods, and it is excessive transpiration of water from the plants that causes the damage.

Partial protection from sun-scald has been obtained through the use of unsightly structures of wood and burlap. More recently scientists have developed an anti-desiccant spray coating which encases the plant leaves in protective plastic "envelopes." This plastic coating is only slightly porous and reduces excessive moisture losses from foliage caused by high temperatures and intense sunlight during the winter.

Anti-desiccant spray is harmless to plants and animals and is quite easy to apply. Since the material will form a protective coating on the sprayer surfaces as well as on plant leaves, it is wise to rinse the spray tank and nozzles to avoid clogging.

Best protection is obtained from two applications. The first should be made just before the winter freeze-up; the second as the freezing-thawing weather begins in spring. When growth starts, the material sloughs off.

17

Plant Hormones Aid Gardening

GEORGE S. AVERY, JR.

PLANT scientists have made fine contributions to horticulture through their work with growth regulators. Many of these chemical aids are available to home gardeners to control fruit set and plant growth and to aid root formation.

The plant hormones recommended for garden use have been tested many times on humans and animals and there is no evidence of their being harmful. These chemicals are obtainable at well-stocked garden supply stores and the manufacturer's directions generally are adequate to explain their proper use.

The following are some of the practical uses to which these substances can be applied:

FRUIT TREES. Apple thinning usually is an onerous task, either in a home-sized orchard or commercial planting. Fruit setting preparations have changed this. By spraying apple trees after full bloom, preferably shortly after petal fall, chemical thinning can be a practical procedure. The end result is a harvest of good-sized apples rather than large numbers of small, poorly developed fruits.

The same preparations can be sprayed on fruit trees such as apples and pears to prevent pre-harvest drop. The timing of these sprays can be a little tricky but the manufacturer's directions are adequate for practical needs.

ORNAMENTALS. Akin to chemical thinning of apples is the complete prevention of fruit set on certain ornamentals that produce objectionable fruits, such as honey locust, horse chestnut, red and silver maple and ailanthus. Fruit-setting sprays are used in this technique, but they are successful only on certain species. They are well worth trying if a tree produces objectionable fall fruits that litter lawns.

BERRIES. There are certain hormones available that are helpful in

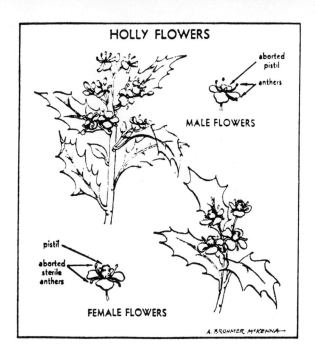

HOLLY FLOWERS

aborted pistil

anthers

MALE FLOWERS

pistil

aborted sterile anthers

FEMALE FLOWERS

A. BROHMER MᶜKENNA

Waxy holly flowers usually appear in May. Berries on female plants can be encouraged by spraying the open flowers with fruit-set hormones. Female blooms are distinguished by the enlarged pistil, and the male flowers by four pollen-bearing anthers. Only the female hollies will produce berries.

producing more individual fruits on berry plants. Sprays can be applied to the open flowers and small newly formed fruits of strawberries, raspberries and blackberries. Bigger and more luscious fruits will be produced and the bearing period will be extended. Holly-berry set can also be achieved. Repeat sprayings at three- or four-day intervals are recommended.

The manufacturer's instructions are based on experimental work done by universities and the United States Department of Agriculture. The home gardener might do this spraying as an experiment and leave a few fruit clusters unsprayed to check results.

TOMATOES. Tomato plants growing in temperate climes bloom for three or four weeks before any fruit is formed. These early flowers always drop from the plant and are wasted because the nights and days are too cool for fruit to set (under 60 degrees). Chemical substitutes for pollination make early fruit set possible. Some of the preparations are available in aerosol cans.

The tomato plants are sprayed when the first two blossoms of a flower cluster are open. The application is repeated every four or five days. These early tomatoes will be seedless and will be ready for harvest at least three weeks before the naturally pollinated fruits.

ROOTING CUTTINGS. The hormone treatment of cuttings is little more than rooting insurance. When preparations are applied to the ends of cuttings, they will induce quicker rooting and more roots. But if cuttings of a species do not ordinarily root under favorable conditions, the treatment will not change the situation. In short, they expedite the process but these hormones cannot switch non-rooting cuttings into those that will produce new root growth easily.

LARGER PLANTS. For reasons difficult to understand, it has long been the desire of many home gardeners to apply a spray to a plant, and in a few days find a plant with blossoms or size that outclass anything previously known. Such aspirations may have been handed down from farmer ancestors who won prizes for the largest watermelons, pumpkins and the like at county fairs. In any case, researchers turned wishful thinking into some surprising facts when they discovered gibberellic acid several years ago.

If the chemical is applied to certain species of plants at particular stages of growth, gibberellic acid can make plants "grow up to three times bigger and faster." For most of us, gibrel is still something for experimentation rather than an established chemical tool to be used for achieving certain desired ends.

1 8

Plants to Attract the Birds

BARBARA B. PAINE

THERE are many hardy, appealing plants that will invite birds to the garden with bright berries and nesting sites.

Top honors go to the Japanese flowering crabapple (*Malus floribunda*). All small-fruited crabapples provide excellent bird fare and they have the additional merits of being decorative for at least two seasons. Also high on the list are the carmine crabapple (*M. atrosanguinea*) and Adam's crabapple (*M. zumi adamsi*).

Other good small trees are the Washington hawthorn (*Crataegus phaenopyrum*), European mountain ash (*Sorbus aucuparia*) and flowering dogwood (*Cornus florida*), each chosen from a genus well known for its popularity with birds. The Washington thorn is especially attractive to winter finches like pine grosbeaks and purple finches, and the mountain ash draws cedar waxwings, catbirds and robins. Fruits of the various dogwoods are eaten by at least eighty-six kinds of birds.

It has been said that if a gardener could choose only one tree to make his land attractive to birds, he would certainly plant a mulberry. The Russian mulberry (*Morus alba tatarica*) is especially worth while, except for the nuisance of fallen fruits.

Among the shrub selections, old reliable Japanese barberry (*Berberis thunbergi*) is ideal. It offers food when it is needed most—during the winter and early spring—and good cover all year round.

Three viburnums are suggested—arrowwood (*Viburnum dentatum*), nannyberry (*V. lentago*) and American cranberry bush (*V. trilobum*). All can stand considerable shade, and between them they probably attract several dozen kinds of birds. Arrowwood is thought to be the favorite of the birds, but the brilliant red fruits of the American cranberry bush make it the most decorative.

Since shrub dogwoods are as popular with both birds and gardeners as their larger-sized relatives, two species are included: Siberian

Birds can be attracted to a property if they have the shelter of near-by trees for a lookout and the fruits of berried shrubs for winter feed. A windowsill feeder, placed where the birds can see it easily, will also attract them during the cold months.

Landscape by Alice Dustan Koller; Molly Adams

dogwood (*Cornus alba*) and gray dogwood (*C. racemosa paniculata*). So, too, with the honeysuckles. Of the many varieties available that attract birds, the red tatarian honeysuckle (*Lonicera tatarica sibirica*) is first choice. A new dwarf species (*L. ruprechtiana* H. V. Clavey Dwarf) looks promising for small home sites.

One unusual suggestion is golden St. Johnswort (*Hypericum frondosum*). It has delightful yellow flowers in the spring and seeds which attract juncos and tree and other sparrows during the winter. Another is northern bayberry (*Myrica pensylvanica*), which grows as well inland as on the seashore.

Evergreens are important for winter interest and wildlife cover. Over fifty kinds of birds eat the fruits of the red cedar (*Juniperus virginiana*) and many nest in its dense, sheltering foliage. The seeds of the Canada hemlock (*Tsuga canadensis*) are eaten by chickadees, nuthatches, juncos, several sparrows and the winter finches like pine siskins and the grosbeaks.

While special plants undoubtedly attract birds, there is no guarantee that they will do so in a particular garden. For instance, no matter how densely planted with dogwoods and honeysuckles, city gardens are not popular with birds except in the migrating seasons.

1 9

A Home Nursery

F. F. ROCKWELL

THE new home owner with a limited budget for landscaping often puts off to the last the purchases that should be made first. If a home nursery were started even before the family actually moved to the new property, money could be saved and a supply of sturdy plants assured.

Even those with little gardening experience can have a plant nursery. No more gardening know-how is required to plant and care for a few young evergreens, trees and shrubs than to grow most annual flowers and vegetables. In fact, with few exceptions, it is easier to grow trees than flowers.

As to the space required, a very small nursery plot—ten feet wide by fifteen or twenty feet long—will accommodate a surprising number of small evergreens and trees. There will even be space for a collection of perennials for propagating, such as iris, daylilies, phlox and chrysanthemums.

Evergreens are a good example of what may be achieved with a home nursery. They may be bought as seedlings or transplants. Seedlings are usually two to four years old and cost five to ten cents each for common species such as Scotch pine, white pine and most spruces. Hemlocks are slightly higher. At these prices, the minimum order from commercial nurseries is usually fifty of a kind, which is more than the average home owner would have use for unless the plants are for hedges. But usually a neighbor or two will be glad to share the order.

Transplants are older than seedlings and have been transplanted once in the nursery. Transplants cost about twice as much as seedlings.

In three to five years these little trees will grow into sizable specimens. They require no care except weeding and watering.

Shrubs, of course, are much less expensive than trees. Nevertheless a shrub border of any size is expensive. Small-sized plants of most shrub species, after one or two years in the home nursery, will be ready to provide an immediate effect when shifted to the garden.

The small area set aside for the home nursery should have good, well-drained soil which has been thoroughly prepared (dug at least one foot deep). Work a generous amount of manure into the soil. Lacking that, turn under a three-inch layer of peat moss, plus balanced fertilizer.

The nursery site should get at least half a day of sun. Equally important is an ample and convenient supply of water, for vigorous growth cannot be expected under drought conditions. Mulching is advisable for most plants. Great care should be exercised with labels, too, for plant names are easily forgotten in a year or two.

One thing more: Buy plants from a reliable dealer. Often they may be procured from a local nursery, although a wider selection of species and varieties may be available from the mail-order firms that specialize in seedlings and transplants (and rooted cuttings) at wholesale.

Trees with Character

DAVID H. ENGEL

WIDE expanses of glass in modern houses bring more of the garden into view. It is important, then, that trees and shrubs have interesting character, especially during winter when many plants are leafless. Specimen plants of unusual form are sometimes called living sculpture.

The idea that plants are living sculpture is not new. The exquisite boxwood topiary of formal English and French gardens are sculptural forms, although they do not relate to the natural appearance of the plant. Topiary is considered as a block of living material to be sheared in whatever shape fancy dictates.

Specimen trees and shrubs are permitted to grow in their natural forms. They are valued as specimens, however, for their flowers or foliage or for the shade they provide. But in the Orient, where beauty of line is emphasized more than mass, a plant is valued for its bare structure and the lines of its branches.

In some plants the sculptural quality of the structure is natural and "built-in," so that only light pruning is needed to maintain the lines. Typical examples are Harry Lauder's walking stick (*Corylus avellana contorta*), Hankow corkscrew willow (*Salix matsudana tortuosa*), silk tree (*Albizzia*), umbrella pine (*Pinus*), Japanese maple, nandina and beach plum. Other plants, with lines hidden by masses of foliage and wood, require severe pruning and a perceptive eye that can see through excess underbrush.

Sometimes nature, in the form of wind, drought, lightning, snow, hail, arrested disease, rugged terrain or old age, does the drastic shaping. The result may be a bent pine on a seacoast or rocky mountainside, a straggling line of gnarled old black willows along a stream bed or a worn-out apple tree in an overgrown orchard. Their beauty is in their structure, a structure which symbolizes the strength they have developed to survive.

Unfortunately such natural sculptured forms are rarely found ready-made in a garden. The gardener, therefore, must either collect them from the wild or buy nursery plants that have possibilities of development. Before the final effect is achieved, the pruning shears will have to be used to reveal the plant's true character. Throughout the life of the plant the gardener-as-artist must guide growth to preserve an ideal proportion and scale of parts.

In selecting a plant for living sculpture, it is better to choose one that is slow growing and that already has an interesting basic structure. Taste must guide selection, too. It is not merely a question of finding a plant with the most erratic or grotesque habit or complex system of branching. Look for a plant that already has achieved an interesting or finished sculptured form through the forces of nature, or one that can be pruned to show simple strength, rhythmic flow of lines, asymmetrical balance or delicate tracery.

In addition to trees already mentioned, others that are adaptable to selective pruning are pines, dogwoods, flowering crabapples and hawthorns. Shrub possibilities include some euonymus varieties, Jap-

A gnarled, windswept pine is a handsome focal point for the foundation planting of a ranch-style house. *John Bickel*

anese holly (*Ilex crenata*), mountain laurel, huckleberry, Japanese andromeda (*Pieris*), Ibota privet (*Ligustrum ibota*), firethorn (*Pyracantha*) and Siebold viburnum.

Size must be considered first in placing the plant in the garden. What is its scale in relationship to adjacent buildings, walls, fences and plants? Color and texture of the background must also be taken into account so that the plant is displayed to best effect. Trees and shrubs with dark-colored bark and foliage should have a background of light-colored material, and vice versa. In the same way, plants of complex or intricate branching should have a plain background.

Sometimes a better effect can be achieved by grouping trees or shrubs of the same species if they appear too weak or insignificant standing alone. Or a plant may form a composition with a rock arrangement or piece of sculpture. The final criterion is that the plant be so much a part of the over-all garden composition that it looks as though it had been there from the very beginning.

2 1

A Few Unusual Narrow-leaved Trees

CLARENCE E. LEWIS

THERE are many unusual narrow-leaved evergreens that can add distinction to the home property. Although some of these plants may not be generally available in nurseries, they are worth a bit of searching.

The true cedars deserve greater use in landscaping. Three species are especially recommended—the Atlas cedar (*Cedrus atlantica*), historic cedar of Lebanon (*C. libani*) and the deodar cedar (*C. deodara*). The Atlas cedar is the hardiest and most easily obtainable of the three.

The blue variety of Atlas cedar (*C. atlantica glauca*), has excellent silver blue, needlelike leaves. It will reach a height of twenty-five feet in about thirty-five years.

The green-needled Atlas cedar and cedar of Lebanon are similar in appearance. They are both branched laterally and make interesting focal points for almost any lawn. Deodar cedar has a looser but very attractive habit, with longer gray needles than the other two cedar species. However, it is not completely hardy in northern climates unless partially protected from prevailing winds. It, too, has a blue-leaved variety that is hardier than the species.

Cedars can be successfully transplanted, although they become increasingly more difficult to move as they grow larger. Good soil drainage is a must for best growth. True cedars are not inexpensive, but they will give the gardener the satisfaction of having top-quality plant material.

An unusual evergreen from Japan that has been in cultivation for about 100 years is the Japanese cryptomeria. This narrow columnar tree attains a height of forty feet around New York City but it may grow to a 100 or more feet in Japan. The foliage resembles that of the big redwood (*Sequoia gigantea*) of California. From a distance the branches and branchlets present a clumplike appearance which is different from that of any other narrow-leaved evergreen.

The red-brown bark of Japanese cryptomeria is somewhat shreddy, adding to the unusual appearance of this somewhat droopy, whip-branched tree. When young it has good density, but with maturity a partial openness develops, although it is not objectionable. A slightly hardier and more clumpy variety is the Lobb cryptomeria. A slow-growing dwarf form is listed as *Cryptomeria japonica nana*.

A narrow-leaved evergreen that in no way resembles any other is the umbrella pine (*Sciadopitys verticillata*). The long, dark green fleshy leaves radiate out at the tips of branches like the stays of an umbrella. This narrow pyramidal tree is seldom taller than twenty-five feet in this country, but will reach 100 feet or more in its native Japan. The umbrella pine has no serious insect or disease problems. In the winter, when planted in shade, the tree's long straplike needles become almost black-green.

An interesting true pine is the bristle-cone pine (*Pinus aristata*), which is slow growing with curved, whiplike branches. It can be grown in a planter or tub. Other pines worth investigating are the lateral-branched, blue form of the Japanese white pine (*Pinus parviflora glauca*), which is suitable for a terrace. The blue-green loose-needled Himalayan pine (*P. griffihi*) has lateral but graceful branching. The lace-bark pine (*P. burgeana*) also is showy. Its mottled bark develops green and tan tones, becoming almost white as the tree matures.

The Spanish fir (*Abies pinsapo*) has radial needles that look as though they were filled with water. Its blue variety also is attractive. These trees are recommended for larger properties rather than for the average home grounds. A spruce that has extremely sharp-pointed, long radial needles is the tiger-tail spruce (*Picea polita*).

The cone-bearing trees that have no leaves during the winter are the dawn redwood (*Metasequoia glyptostroboides*) and the golden larch (*Pseudolarix amabilis*). Dawn redwood was known only as a fossil for many years, but in the mid-forties it was discovered in the northeastern Hupeh Province of China. It is now sold by several nurseries. The tree is quite hardy; the foliage resembles that of our Southern bald cypress.

A large horizontally branched tree, the golden larch has beautiful leaves that turn yellow in early fall. The new leaves that appear in spring are a fresh rich green.

2 2

Small Trees with Flowers

ROBERT B. CLARK

SMALL flowering trees are ideally suited to the average-sized suburban property. If they are placed properly and selected wisely, they can provide bright accents of seasonal bloom during late winter, spring, summer and even early fall.

A few warm days in March will bring out the yellow flower clusters of the Cornelian cherry (*Cornus mas*). If the weather remains cool, the flowers last for about a month, a display that is more subtle than the bright, sometimes garish forsythia.

The Cornelian cherry's shrublike tendency can be overcome if the young plant is trained to one or two stems. Then it will develop into a tree form and grow twelve to fifteen feet tall.

The foliage of this dogwood species is neat, smooth-margined and dark glossy green. In July, short-stemmed cherrylike red fruits appear among the leaves but they are eaten quickly by birds. The red autumn foliage drops in October to reveal budded stems.

Another early-flowering, small tree is the Kobus magnolia from Japan. White-petaled, faintly scented flowers cover the gray, leafless branches in mid to late April. Hardy, this magnolia is at its best in an open spot. In a protected place the tree may bloom too early and the flowers would be browned by late frosts. The pink-flowered saucer magnolia (*M. soulangeana*) is later blooming.

For a shower of deep pink bloom when the grass is new, few small trees can equal the weeping Higan cherry (*Prunus subhirtella pendula*). The blossoms may be featured against the somber backdrop of spruce, pine or hemlock. This graceful tree will grow wherever peaches succeed. There is a double-flowering form which remains in bloom longer than the common type. Often rather washed-out pink forms are offered for sale and the gardener would do well to visit a reliable nursery when the trees are in bloom before ordering his own plants.

Amanogawa, which means "Milky Way," is a narrow columnar form of the oriental flowering cherry. The blooms are double, pale bluish. The smooth, red-toned bark and unfolding red leaves make an

The loose, hanging clusters of the fringe tree appear during the warm summer months.

Gottscho-Schleisner

Japanese flowering dogwood is a dramatic tree which blooms in summer when the leaves are full.

Paul E. Genereux

enchanting setting for them. Since this cherry has emphatic vertical lines, it can accentuate a grouping or be used instead of Lombardy poplars where space is limited.

A springtime snowstorm is suggested by the crabapples. There are many kinds, usually spreading in habit. They are of medium to low stature (fifteen to thirty feet tall), and white or pink in bloom. Commonest in the Eastern states is the Japanese flowering crab (*Malus floribunda*). New selections now are available including Katherine, a double white, and Dorothea, a double pink.

America's contribution to springtime beauty is the flowering dogwood (*Cornus florida*). The notched white showy bracts are abundant on the wide spreading branches. They last for about two weeks in early May, before the leaves appear. These trees rarely reach twenty feet in height.

The Japanese species (*C. kousa*) extends the dogwood blooming season well into June. The square-pointed flowers appear after the leaves have unfolded, creating a startling effect of summer snow above the bright green leaves.

Fragrant, feathery white clusters of flowers are featured in late May and early June by the white fringe tree (*Chionanthus virginicus*). The male blooms are showier. Like holly, the fringe tree requires pollination by the flowers of another tree in order to produce the olivelike berries which are deep blue, but not very showy. The foliage of the fringe tree is handsome but coarse, so the tree is best placed by itself.

With its ranks of fringed white petals that recall the shoulder ornaments of Civil War soldiers, the epaulette tree (*Pterostyrax hispida*) can be a conversation piece in any sheltered garden spot during late May. The fresh green foliage expands just as the pendant flower clusters appear. In July the fuzzy fruits develop.

Another attractive May-blooming member of the storax (styrax family is the white-clustered silverbell tree (*Halesia carolina*). The branchlets of both trees bear shreddy bark.

Summer-blooming trees are few in number but three are notable: stewartia, sourwood and the Chinese scholar tree. The first two are native to the Southern Appalachian Mountains.

The mountain stewartia (*S. ovata*) bears cup-shaped white flowers a few at a time during July. Inside the glistening petals of each flower is a fringe of orange stamens. Glossy green leaves make a handsome setting for the blooms. The variety *S. ovata grandiflora*, called the showy stewartia, has larger flowers with purple stamens. An oriental species, *S. koreana*, has brown bark that flakes off to reveal green and pink inner bark. Stewartias often have several trunks. Since stewartias come from southern climates, they respond to a sheltered situation in northern gardens.

A hardier Southerner is the sourwood or sorrel tree (*Oxydendrum arboreum*). It has peachlike foliage and lily-of-the-valleylike flowers. Flaring strings of white bell-like blooms appear at the tips of branches in midsummer. A display lasts for several weeks while the flowers change into straw-colored fruits that remain showy during the fall foliage season. Sourwood's autumn leaves rival those of sour gum or pepperidge in earliness and glory of color.

Summer heat and drought seem easier to take if there is a Chinese scholar tree (*Sophora japonica*) on the property. This medium-sized tree provides welcome shade and refreshing color with its shiny green foliage and clusters of pale yellow flowers. A member of the pea family, it thrives in hot dry situations. The scholar tree is the largest species of hardy flowering trees and one of the last to bloom.

2 3

Fruit Tree Espalier

HENRY P. LEUTHARDT

ESPALIERED or trained fruit trees are filling important roles in landscaping by providing design and color for contemporary gardens. The meticulously trimmed branches form leafy patterns against buildings and fences with added features of spring bloom and fall fruit.

Espalier training is based on several horticultural principles. When understood, it is easier to plan tree care. Symmetry of pattern is of utmost importance. An even flow of sap aids in the development of bearing fruit spurs.

The open exposure of the plants to sunlight results in large fruit. Tree varieties must be selected carefully, since certain kinds grow best in horizontally trained shapes while others thrive when trained vertically. Proper understocks must be used for espalier; a small root system is desired. Also, the proper understock limits the size of the tree by slowing its growth and encouraging early bearing.

There are several basic espalier forms. Palmette Verrier is used only for trees with symmetrical shape without a middle branch issuing from the main trunk. This is true mainly of apples and pears. The Palmette Verrier consists of parallel upright branches and was named for the French university professor who developed the form in the nineteenth century. He believed that upright training contributed immensely to symmetry and production. The Palmette Goucher espalier is distinguished from the Verrier in that it consists of several U-shaped arms in two-fold, three-fold or four-fold espaliers.

The horizontal cordons are recommended for those fruit varieties which have a natural drooping tendency such as Yellow Delicious apple or Bosc pear. The cordon consists of one, two, three or more tiers of long branches trained fifteen to eighteen inches apart. The English use the fan shaped pattern widely throughout their gardens. Peaches, nectarines, cherries as well as apples and pears grow well in this pattern.

Pruning, spraying, proper support and fertilization are essential to espalier care. The espaliered trees must be supported to prevent the branches from being blown by the wind or broken under the weight of the fruit. A wooden trellis may be built in the basic form of the espalier. Wire fastened three to six inches away from a wall also

Lush spring growth on an espaliered apple tree should be thinned out in summer.

Sy Friedman

A triple-U espalier is pruned back to tidy four-inch shoots, leaving fruit buds to develop.

Sy Friedman

TOP LEFT: If there is a fruit bud on an espaliered tree shoot, cut the stem about two inches above it.

TOP RIGHT: Cutting of a shoot above a potential bud will encourage the fruit to develop.

RIGHT: A latent fruit bud, which appeared last year, bears young apples for harvest.

Sy Friedman

may be used. To tie the tree to the support, raffia or plastic strips should be used. Wire or string is not recommended since they would cut into the bark as the tree grows. A tree that is supported properly will retain its original shape.

Pruning will maintain the shape of the tree and rid it of excessive growth. Pruning also develops fruit buds and bearing spurs. Apples and pears bear primarily on spurs. Peaches and nectarines bear fruit on one-year-old shoots. A bearing spur is a shoot or twig of limited growth with short internodes (distances between the leaves).

Espaliers are pruned at least twice a year—during the summer in June and once during the winter. The winter pruning is done to cut out dead wood and excessive shoots.

Summer pruning helps to keep the plant in its proper shape. Espaliered fruit trees have sent out shoots mainly from the point at which the arms connect with the trunk. These shoots should be pruned back flush with the trunk and arms or pruned to encourage fruit bud formation. When an espalier has reached the desired height, it is easily kept at that height by pruning the tops of the vertical branches.

Fruit buds are made or differentiated in late June and continue developing throughout the summer. A latent fruit bud is a bud with four or five leaves around it. A leaf bud is found under the axil of a single leaf. If the shoot on which the fruit bud appears is pruned an inch or two above the latent fruit bud, this bud will develop into a fruit bud.

Occasionally a tree will shoot out excessively after it has been pruned in June. These shoots may have to be cut back again during the summer if growing conditions are extremely favorable. All shoots should be kept to about four inches. Since peaches bear fruit primarily on one-year-old shoots, some of these shoots should be left for next year's fruit. A peach is very vegetative, however, and it is best to remove one-third to one-half of last year's shoots during the winter.

A good spray program is essential to good fruit. Scale, scab, aphid and leaf hoppers are the principal pests in apples. Pear psylla, scale blister mite and fire blight attack pears. Peaches and nectarines are susceptible to brown rot, red leaf curl and peach borer. Most of the pests are controlled with the application of miscible oil during the dormant period, and one of the general-purpose fruit sprays should give sufficient protection during the summer. For specific controls of pear psylla, sprays should be applied at the end of July and during August. A spray of malathion applied to the trunk and branches of peach trees from mid-July to mid-August should control the peach borer.

2 4

Twelve Nearly Perfect Trees

RAYMOND P. KORBOBO

WHAT makes a tree perfect for the home property? Ideally, it should have a graceful appearance at all seasons, fine foliage, attractive flowers, good fall color, interesting bark, a strong branching habit,

A planting pocket left in the broad terrace paving provides space for a pin oak to shade the outdoor living area.

Landscape by William A. Rutherford; Gottscho-Schleisner

deep roots, resistance to ice and wind damage, and a wide tolerance of soils. In addition, the perfect tree should be free of insects and disease and should withstand dry spells, severe winters and the rigors of transplanting.

Obviously, the gardener's dream tree does not exist. But there are an even dozen that, in my opinion, come extremely close to perfection.

The Chinese scholar tree (*Sophora japonica*) is a truly beautiful tree. It has more width than height and its branching habit resembles that of the elm. Foliage is refined, with many leaflets per leaf, and flowers appear in August. It is strong and practically free of insects and disease.

The pin oak (*Quercus palustris*) is a true veteran. In its favor are refined foliage, availability, ease of transplanting, rapid growth, good fall color, strong branching habit and tough wood. Pin oak is one of the best choices for wet soil. The scarlet oak (*Q. coccinea*) has identical virtues, plus another advantage: pruning is less of a chore.

Professional arborists can find a lively topic in the relative hardiness of the willow oak, an unusual, refined species. A safe hardiness limit would be an imaginary line from New York City through Easton, Pennsylvania. North of this line there is spotty evidence that the tree is not reliably hardy. The growth pattern of the willow oak resembles that of the pin oak, while its foliage resembles that of the willow. The tree, at any age, is something to admire.

The ginkgo or maidenhair tree (*Ginkgo biloba*) is the perfect shade tree—with one exception. It refuses to become handsome in any-

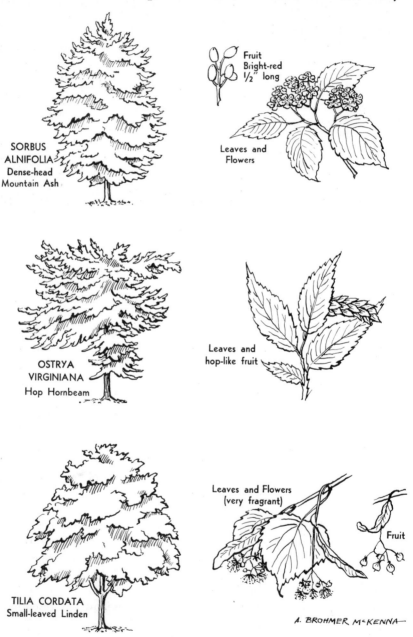

These three shade trees are suitable for small properties.

thing less than eighteen or twenty years. The form and fan-shaped foliage of this living fossil are unique. It is completely free of insects and disease. Gardeners should buy male plants only. The female forms are ugly ducklings, for their ripened fruits have an offensive odor that makes them unwelcome.

Sweet gum (*Liquidambar styraciflua*) is another fine shade tree that will do well in a wet location. The five-lobed leaves are star-shaped. In the fall their rich purples and reds are unmatched. Many plants tend to form a twin trunk, which is sometimes a needed break from the monotony of all perfectly straight trunks. If the sweet gum has a serious demerit, it would be seed burrs in the lawn. However, they create no problem if the lawn is raked clean in early spring.

Honey locust (*Gleditsia triacanthos inermis* Shademaster) is, except for the *Sophora*, perhaps the most graceful tree there is. Filtered shade is its strongest feature. At the present time, all of the honey locusts pose a possible insect control problem. Some are susceptible; some are not. In spite of this failing, I still feel it belongs among the best.

The maples almost missed this list. The troubles that accompany these trees could make a full-length article. However, the beautiful bark and breathtaking fall color of the sugar maple (*Acer saccharum*) forces me to include it.

Certain smaller trees belong on the dozen-best list. Some day Japanese silverbell (*Styrax japonica*) will rival the magnolias, crab-apples and cherries in popularity. In early June the tree is almost covered with delicate, white, pendulous, bell-shaped flowers with clear yellow centers. It is fast growing, tolerant, strong and even does well in partial shade.

The golden rain tree (*Koelreuteria paniculata*) is a medium-sized tree with beautiful clusters of golden-yellow flowers in midsummer. Seed pods add interest for many more weeks. In the same height

1. Chinese scholar tree. 2. American hornbeam. 3. Sweet gum. 4. Golden rain tree. 5. Pin oak. 6. Ginkgo. 7. Scarlet oak. 8. Willow oak. 9. Japanese silverbell. 10. Flowering crabapple. 11. Sugar maple. 12. Honey locust.

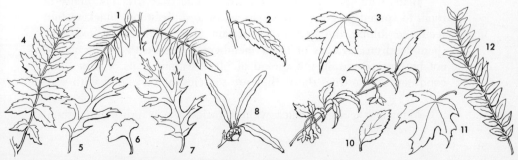

category are the flowering crabapples. The varieties are too numerous to mention—they are best inspected at first hand when trees are in bloom.

Rounding out the list is the American hornbeam (*Carpinus caroliniana*). Many people feel that if a small tree does not have conspicuous flowers, it is worthless. Here is a native of this area so tough and interesting that it needs no bright flowers to captivate gardeners. The American hornbeam, among small trees, comes as close to the ideal tree as *Sophora* does in the large tree group.

2 5

Nut Trees to Grow in the Suburbs

MAURICE BROOKS

NUT-BEARING trees, either native or introduced, are handsome accents for the home property. Some species are among the largest and most beautiful of the shade trees. Furthermore, the harvesting of nuts can be a lively autumn pastime for the family.

Deservedly the most popular of native eastern nut trees is the black walnut (*Juglans nigra*). Its botanical range extends from Maine to Texas, although the tree reaches its best growth in the rich alluvial soils of the Ohio and Mississippi valleys. In the Northeast *J. nigra* will succeed in almost any fertile soil that is deep enough for its extensive taproot.

Black walnut is splendid as a lawn shade tree, if it has plenty of room to spread its crown. For reasons little understood, black walnut seems to inhibit the growth of certain other plants. For example, rhododendrons, azaleas or other members of the heath family should not be planted within the spread of black walnut roots. Under some conditions apple trees die if they are too closely associated with walnuts.

Many horticultural black walnut varieties now are being propa-

gated. Of these, perhaps the best is Thomas. Over a long period of
time it has proved to have more desirable characteristics over a wider
geographical range and in more varied soils than any other variety.
Thomas grows rapidly and vigorously. It begins bearing at an early
age. The nuts are of superior flavor and have good cracking qualities.
Stambaugh and Ohio are other superior varieties.

White walnut or butternut (*J. cinerea*) is another native tree of
great value. It reaches its best growth somewhat farther north than
does black walnut. Ordinarily, butternut does not reach the size of
black walnut. *J. cinerea* produces particularly rich and flavorful nuts.
The shells are rather thick, and the kernels are difficult to remove.
Established varieties include Sherwood and Buckley.

Introduced walnut species for Northeastern planting include
Persian or English walnut (*J. regia*) and heartnut (*J. sieboldiana
cordiformis*). Persian walnut succeeds as far north as southern New
England, while heartnut thrives northward to southern Canada.

Persian walnuts are best planted on an experimental basis in the
East. They prefer limestone soils and should be given sheltered locations. Heartnuts are much hardier; their flavor compares with butter-
nuts.

Close relatives of the walnuts are the native hickories. The most
popular species is the pecan (*Carya illinoensis*). The best northern
hickories are the shagbarks (*C. ovata*) and the shellbarks (*C. lacini-
osa*). Both species produce nuts of fine quality, although kernels are
difficult to extract. Among the superior named varieties are Stratford,
Glover and Fairbanks.

Pecans grow into attractive small trees as far north as Long
Island, although they do not always produce crops. Major and Green-
river are good varieties for northern plantings. Promising hybrids between pecans and northern hickories, called "hicans," now are available.

The best available substitute for the vanished American chestnut
is the blight-resistant Chinese chestnut (*Castanea mollissima*). This
species is treelike southward, but often is shrubby north of the Middle
Atlantic states. It produces nuts of good flavor and is an early bearer.
Young trees require constant moisture during the growing season.

The American filbert or hazel (*Corylus americana*) is a hardy
shrub that bears flavorful nuts. Crops are borne irregularly, however,
and nuts are smaller than those of the European filbert (*C. avellana*).
Many varieties of this introduced species have been tried in the
Northeast, usually with indifferent success. Most filberts bloom too
early for cold springs.

A superior American filbert, the Rush variety, has been used extensively to hybridize with European filberts. The most promising results of this hybridization is the Bixby variety, usually a reliable bearer of good nuts. Filberts are self-sterile and must be planted with other varieties if they are to produce crops.

Most nut-bearing trees have very long taproots and must, therefore, be planted in deep, well-drained soils. Abundant organic matter is a prerequisite for success. Since trees in good situations grow quite large, they must not be crowded.

Gardeners who plan to use a few nut trees in their home plantings should obtain named varieties from specialty nurseries. First costs will be higher, but results are almost certain to be better.

2 6

Planting Deciduous Trees

P. L. RUSDEN

ONE of the most rewarding experiences for a suburbanite with a house lot of moderate size is to select, plant and cultivate a deciduous tree. When it comes to do-it-yourself projects, however, the home owner will find that his limit will be reached rather soon in doing this. Size is a limiting factor. With size goes weight—a lot of it. If the tree cannot be brought home in the station wagon, you might just as well leave the whole job to a professional tree mover. Do not be discouraged by the fact that the tree you can plant successfully is not very impressive in size. It will be, and sooner than you think.

Is it to be a shade tree, ornamental or both? Spring flowers? Bright fall foliage? Nurserymen will help make a selection. A nursery is a much better source than Uncle Ned's farm in Dutchess County, for the nurseryman will have root-pruned the tree and in other ways adapted it to lead a civilized life. The farm woodlot tree is not so adapted.

For the sake of simplicity, suppose the choice is a sugar maple that calipers 2½ to 3 inches just above the flare where the tree trunk leaves the ground. The tree will be about 12 to 14 feet high above the roots. The roots may come in a burlap-wrapped ball of soil or they may be bare. In either case they must not be allowed to dry out. The balled and burlaped tree is safer to handle. Though it will be quite heavy, it will tend to stand by itself while being positioned. As to planting time, two periods are favored by the professionals: fall when trees are dormant, but while the soil is still workable; spring before tree buds are open, but when the soil has dried out enough to be worked. After fall planting it is especially worthwhile to lay a good mulch of chips, marsh grass, leafmold or peat moss over the root area to reduce the chance of frost heaving if the winter turns out to be severely cold with inadequate snow cover.

There is an old saying among arborists and nurserymen that if you have ten dollars to spend on a tree, spend two dollars for the tree and eight dollars for the hole. A carefully prepared site, then, is worth at the outset about four times as much as the tree. The idea is to give the tree the best possible start in its new role.

Dig deeply—deep enough to have a margin of space below the largest root or below the bottom of the root ball if the tree is burlapped. Discard all the rocks and any trash while excavating. For clay soil that does not drain well, dig down a couple of extra feet and fill just this extra space with small rocks or very coarse gravel. This improves soil drainage under the root system.

For a small tree with a two-foot ball, dig a hole four feet across and three feet deep. Line the hole with a generous amount of good topsoil and peat moss. Put enough of the mixture in the hole to bring the tree up to its original level with respect to the final grade. In all probability there will be a light area on the bark just above the root ball that will mark where the ground level was in the nursery. Never plant deeper than this. A little less deep is even better.

Place the tree carefully in the hole with the trunk vertical. If the roots are bare, they should be gently and carefully spread out by a helper while you steady the trunk. Roots started out at a wrong angle or crowded so as to turn back on themselves will eventually cause trouble. Do not position the tree by rotating it unless the roots are straightened at the same time. In years to come, a root that has a tendency to grow around the trunk may succeed in strangling the tree.

As soil is returned to fill any spaces left between the root system of the tree and the sides of the hole, the soil should be watered in. It is important not to have any air pockets under the root system. Tree roots will not grow into air pockets. The soil should be tamped into place with a stick (a hoe handle will do) as the filling progresses. The resulting firming of the soil will largely eliminate the settling of the tree later.

Do not add fertilizer when the tree is planted. There will be time later when it has become established.

A small tree properly planted should be braced against the toppling effect of winds. Wire guys fastened to pegs in the ground and encased in short lengths of old garden hose where they go around the tree trunk give good support. Three will do the job if placed at appropriate angles. They should be left in place for about a year or until the tree can stand alone.

"Thin skinned" trees, maples and beeches, for example, may be protected from sunscald and frost during their first year on a new site by wrapping the trunk with a spiral of tree paper or burlap.

Where a mulch is used, it should not be piled high around the base of the trunk. Rodents may nest in a deep mulch in the winter and girdle the tree by feeding on the bark. In the case of fruit trees, flowering crabapples, young dogwoods etc., it is well to place a barrier of hardware cloth (galvanized one-half-inch mesh wire screening) about two feet high around the base of the trunk. This will discourage rodents from feeding on the bark under the snow or on top of the snow. In some parts of northern New York and New England fruit growers use hardware cloth cylinders four feet high.

A useful device developed by two shrewd Pennsylvania Dutchmen (Naaman Keyser and Edgar Rex) for watering new trees consists of a series of cardboard cylinders about two feet long buried at intervals around the edge of the planting hold. The cylinders are sunk flush with the sod level and filled with coarse bluestone gravel. Through them the roots may be watered quite effectively for the important early seasons while the tree is becoming established.

Making a "saucer" by building a little dam of topsoil around the outer edge of the planting site is a trick frequently used to aid in watering newly planted trees. Never make the mistake of planting the tree in a saucerlike depression to be filled in later. This is one way to start a process of root burial that is harmful. Root burial is especially harmful to dogwoods.

While these planting directions were outlined for a typical sugar maple, they apply equally to other maples, dogwoods, beeches, oaks, tulips, apples, flowering crabs, hawthorns or for that matter almost any tree.

2 7

Tree Pruning

HARRY W. DENGLER

OF all gardening practices, tree pruning is probably the least understood and the most neglected. Yet, few outdoor tasks can be more productive and rewarding than a good pruning job well planned and well carried out.

There is nothing mysterious nor magical involved in pruning trees. All that is needed is a simple appreciation of how trees grow, flower and fruit. The whys, hows and whens will follow naturally.

Trees form buds along their branches during the summer. These remain dormant until the following spring and develop into new leaves and shoots. These buds do not occur haphazardly but are arranged in a precise pattern around each branch. Their closeness to one another depends upon the species of the tree and the vigor of the summer growth on which they were formed. Buds occur singly, in pairs, or rarely, in whorls of three; all point outward from the branch and indicate the direction in which the new shoots will eventually grow.

If a branch is clipped back to just above a bud, its outward or upward growth is stopped at this point and the new direction that the branch will now take is that in which the bud is pointed. Thus the pruner can guide the growth of his trees. If started while the trees are young, pruning will control—within reasonable limits—their ultimate size and form, guiding growth into small or large, tight or open, compact or loose, formal or informal habits.

Overcrowding, dense shade, insects, disease or injuries frequently cause the ends of branches to die. Injured or dead wood should be cut back to just above that outermost, viable bud where a new shoot can grow upwards, downwards or to either side to fill in the gap.

Nearby branches may or may not need to be clipped back to shape the tree. If the tree is too dense, the branch might be removed

Established sapling ready for pruning.

Undesirable branches are removed by initial pruning.

Proof of proper pruning is shown in plant form in July.

Six years later tree shows symmetry and balance.

Davey Tree Expert Co.

completely (to the trunk) to allow more sunlight to penetrate into the foliage. When either of these measures is taken, it is sometimes necessary to clip off and to remove branches in other parts of the tree to provide for balance, natural symmetry or to make the tree grow into the form that the pruner has in mind.

This basic principle of pruning applies equally to twigs and branches. To control or alter the shape of the tree, cut back to the bud, twig or branch that grows in the direction you wish the plant to grow.

A high-quality hand pruner is essential; anything else is an abomination. It can well be a lifetime investment, which should be selected as carefully as a new pair of shoes. The pruner should be reasonably light in weight, sturdy and comfortable in hand. Women gardeners and those with small hands should select a smaller model or one with settings that permit adjustment of the spread of the handles. The proper kind will make pruning more pleasurable and less fatiguing.

All pruning cuts should be made as close as possible to a branch, twig or to the trunk, leaving no stub. Such wounds will heal rapidly providing there is no bark injury. Any cut one-inch in diameter—the size of a quarter—or larger should be painted with an approved wound dressing. An asphalt varnish containing an antiseptic is considered best. When pruning to a bud, the cut should never be made crossways but at an angle of 45 degrees or more, one eighth to one quarter of an inch beyond and sloping away from the bud. The cutting blade of the pruner should always lie flat along the trunk or branch when removing any twigs or shoots.

Trees that set flower buds one summer and produce blossoms the following year are best pruned immediately following the blooming period. If these are pruned in the fall, winter or early spring prior to blooming, the flower buds will be cut off and the number of blooms reduced proportionately to the number of branches removed. Trees in this group include catalpa, eastern dogwood, flowering crabapple, cherry, hawthorn, plum, fringe tree, golden rain tree, lilac, paulownia, eastern and Chinese redbud, spring-flowering magnolia and yellowwood.

The American hollies can be safely pruned anytime until new leaves and shoots appear since their flowers and eventually their berries (on the female plants) are borne on the new growth. The English and Chinese hollies, however, must be pruned with caution, for the flower buds have already set on last summer's branches. Any cutting will reduce the winter crop of berries and the number of pollen-producing flowers on the male plants.

The birch, dogwood, elm, maple, walnut and yellowwood trees are called "bleeders," because they exude excessive amounts of sap from pruning wounds made in late winter and early spring. For this reason they are often pruned after the leaves are fully formed in late spring or early summer. This bleeding is not especially harmful to trees. With "bleeders," it is wisest to make light prunings over a period of years rather than a heavy cutting at any one time.

When young trees are newly planted, there is always some injury to their roots no matter how carefully they may have been handled. Root injury reduces the intake of moisture and nutrients from the soil and requires that the top and root system be put back into balance by removing or clipping off some of the branches and twigs. With the exception of white birches and other trees grown as clumps, the trunks should be trained to single stems and the weaker of any double leaders removed. Smaller and injured side branches should be pruned or shortened in preference to others.

Side branches that form a wide, open angle to the trunk should be favored. Remove those that are narrow and V-shaped. The latter will eventually develop into tight, weak crotches, which might split in heavy winds or when laden with wet snows or ice. Also, narrow crotches collect dirt, debris and moisture, providing easy entrance for decay. This attention to pruning trees while young combined with periodic corrective prunings as they become older will eliminate expensive work in later years.

Large tree limbs are deceptively heavy, awkward and dangerous to remove without the proper equipment, hand tools and some skill. These large branches must be cut up eventually for hauling, so it is often most practical to cut them into short, easily handled lengths while still on the trees.

Work inward from the ends of these limbs toward the trunk. Large limbs are best removed by stub cuttings to prevent splitting and damage to the trunk. This involves an undercut on the branch about one to two feet beyond the trunk and upwards until the pruning saw just barely begins to be pinched. Make a downward cut several times farther out until the limb is severed. With all the weight removed, the stub can be cut safely, making it flush and smooth to the trunk.

2 8

Tree Feeding

EDWARD J. DUDA

AUTUMN is an ideal time to feed trees. When leaves are gone, roots are active; they continue to absorb nutrients until the ground freezes and moisture is locked in the soil. Feeding may also be done during a January thaw, and warm periods in February. Another excellent feeding time is early spring.

Feeding is of prime importance to keep trees vigorous. A well-fed tree will be better able to withstand insect attack, disease and unfavorable environmental changes.

Most lawn trees grow in an environment devoid of the forest ground cover or litter that is so essential for good tree growth. Removal of grass clippings, dead twigs and branches and fallen leaves from the lawn area beneath shade trees means an annual loss of certain mineral elements that would normally be restored to the soil. Unless these elements are provided a tree may begin to show signs of gradual decline over a period of years.

Trees that are not growing properly send up "feed me" signals. There are at least four such indicators that can be clearly observed: Sparse foliage; leaves that are paler green and smaller than normal; die back in the crown, first evidenced in the tips of twigs; and abnormally slow growth. Reduced tree vigor is also indicated by a reduction in the size of growth rings, shortened twig growth and the production of smaller than normal buds.

Although there may be many reasons for decline in trees, poor soil is frequently the primary cause. Tree troubles can usually be traced to the soil's degree of fertility and porosity, its texture, moisture and drainage. Weakness induced by nutrient deficiencies in the soil can make a tree vulnerable to attack by a number of wood-boring insects or diseases.

The soil mass in which tree roots develop is often restricted by driveways, walks and buildings. This is especially true with street trees; the soil may be incapable of supporting good tree growth. Soil in new housing developments may also be inferior. Grade changes have been made and the water table has been altered.

Beneath a few inches of the topsoil there may be a foot or more of sand, clay or fill over what was once a marsh or ravine. Construction debris, such as pieces of board and lath or chips of concrete or plaster which had been bulldozed over when the lawn was put in, scarcely makes a good soil foundation in which to plant shade trees.

When soil is poor, feeding becomes important. The feeding process contributes to aeration, the opening up of hard compacted soils

To feed a tree, the home gardener can use a crowbar to punch 12 to 18-inch deep holes, 2 to 3 feet apart, in the soil area around the trunk. This permits application of fertilizer near the tree root zone. Holes are made in accordance with recommended pattern (inset) in which "A" indicates the tree's main stem, "B" the inner ring of heavy roots, "C" the terminal end of the branches and "D" the outer ring of fine feeder roots. Fertilizer is poured into holes between "B" and "D."

Bartlett Tree Experts; Roche

to make them more porous. But more important, feeding puts into the soil in the area of the feeding roots nutrients that a tree requires for proper growth.

Homeowners can often feed their own trees. They must be equipped, of course, with a crowbar and some fundamental knowledge; they should know when, where and at what depth the tree food should be placed, and in what amount.

A tree absorbs nutrients in soluble form through its feeding roots. Feeding roots are not the thick roots connected to the trunk; these are for storage, anchorage and conduction. Outright absorption is made possible by microscopic root hairs found on the small roots or rootlets.

The majority of these rootlets are located in the area of ground beginning at the drip line or outer periphery of the crown and extending back three fourths the distance to the trunk. They may also be found out beyond the drip line. In gardens it is not uncommon to find wayward roots running 10, 20 or 30 feet or more into a flower bed or some other area rich in nutrients or with adequate moisture. The location in which tree food should be placed should coincide with that area in which the majority of feeding roots are found (as shown in the illustration).

With this location circumscribed, the next step is to prepare holes for the tree food. A crowbar is the best tool. Many tree companies use power augers which drill feeding holes quickly and easily. Each hole should be approximately 2 to 3 feet apart. On a lawn, cut out a circular section of turf and put it aside before making the feeding hole.

The hole should be 12 to 18 inches deep depending on the species of tree. Fill the hole with tree food to within 3 inches of the top. Sprinkle a layer of topsoil over the tree food, replace the plug of turf and tamp down. This will insure against grass burning around the hole. The entire area should then be watered thoroughly to aid flushing of nutrients to the root area.

A highly organic, well-balanced tree food (6-8-6) is recommended: The first number denotes the percentage of nitrogen (to increase rate of cell growth and help produce healthy foliage, twigs and wood); the second is the percentage of phosphoric acid (to aid in root growth and in making stored carbohydrates available for growth next spring); and the third indicates the percentage of potash (to help the storage of starches and to strengthen, toughen and ripen the wood).

Most shade trees should be fed once a year. The amount of tree food for a single tree will vary from 3 to 10 pounds for every inch of trunk diameter at breast height (depending on the tree's vigor). A tree growing more vigorously than another will require less tree food per inch of diameter.

Feeding trees with a liquid fertilizer is a practice followed by many tree companies. This method usually involves high-powered equipment and for this reason it is not advocated for the do-it-your-self homeowner. Nutrients in liquid form are pumped into the soil in the vicinity of the tree roots so that they become quickly available to the tree. Liquid feeding is also achieved by applying essential nutrients directly to the foliage during the growing season. Foliage feeding is necessary where trees are growing in locations that would make it difficult to feed them by any other means.

29

Increase Plants with Tree and Shrub Cuttings

R. R. THOMASSON

PROPAGATING plants in the home garden by means of cuttings or layering is a practical phase of gardening. Home propagation can come to the rescue when the budget for nursery stock is exhausted. Also, it is possible to trade favorite plants with a neighbor.

Some woody plants are difficult to propagate. However, many of the common shrubs may be readily increased from cuttings or layering. I have started pussy willow, red-twigged dogwood, bush honeysuckle, euonymus, forsythia, mockorange and numerous others by merely sticking cuttings eight or ten inches long into ordinary garden soil.

Those who were too busy to take cuttings in the spring have a second chance in the summer. For summer propagation softwood cuttings are taken. This is wood of the current season's growth which is firm enough to break under pressure with a snap. I make the cuttings two to six inches long; the bottom cut is just below a node or leaf bud. If more than one cutting is made from the same stem, the top cut should be just above a node. Always keep cuttings moist until they are set in the rooting medium.

The cuttings may be rooted in sand, vermiculite or a mixture of sand and peat moss. This medium may be placed in a coldframe, box, flower pot or in a special bed in the garden. Humidity is important. Also, cuttings need protection from the midday sun.

To insure uniform humidity, a covering of polyethylene plastic is a great help. Three or four stiff wires are fastened over the box of rooting medium after the manner of the "bows" on a covered wagon. A sheet of polyethylene is then folded over the wires and under the box to make it reasonably airtight. The plastic keeps moisture in but allows gases to escape.

For plants that do not root readily, such as magnolia and holly, the use of one of the root-promoting hormone chemicals is desirable. Follow directions on the package.

Since soil moisture is vital, it is well to start the cuttings where they may be easily reached with the hose. A generous mixture of peat moss or compost in the soil, plus a mulch of the same material, will help hold the moisture.

Many a splendid rosebush has been grown from a cutting taken from a bouquet and stuck in the ground with a glass jar turned upside down over it. A blossom stem four to six inches long with three nodes makes the best cutting. Some shade and ample moisture are essential. While rose cuttings can be rooted in ordinary soil, they will have a better chance in a medium of sphagnum moss or sand and peat moss.

The gardener should not lose sight of the fact, however, that rosebushes purchased from a nursery are more vigorous than the ones that grow on their own roots. Nursery plants are budded or grafted onto strong understocks such as the rugosa, multiflora and dog rose.

Another popular method of increasing plants in the home garden is layering. Cut a vigorous young branch or shoot partway through, bend it down and cover it with an inch or two of soil. I mix peat moss with the soil to improve the moisture-holding capacity. The cut area of the stem will produce roots. Then the new plant can be severed from the parent branch and planted separately in the garden.

1: In May, after the azaleas have flowered, six-inch cuttings are taken from the new growth. The cut is made below a node.

2: Root inducing hormone powder speeds propagation. The cut ends are dipped into the powder and excess is tapped off.

5: The flat is tightly sealed and set in a shaded site for eight to ten weeks. Additional watering should not be necessary.

6: Of the twelve azalea cuttings inserted in the flat, nine developed fibrous roots in eight weeks. Other evergreens are propagated similarly.

A variation on this method is air layering, an ancient Chinese system. It is especially useful for tree and shrub cuttings which do not strike roots readily. Cut partway through the branch and wrap a ball of damp sphagnum moss around the cut. The ball of moss is then wrapped in polyethylene which is tied at each end to make it as nearly airtight as possible.

In considering inexpensive ways of increasing plants at home, do not overlook the pleasure of planting seed gathered on hikes through

3: Treated cuttings are placed into a clean flat containing a half-sand and half-peat mixture. It is soaked the day before planting.

4: The entire flat is covered with a sheet of polyethylene which is supported by arched wires. Moisture is retained.

7: Rooted cuttings are planted in pots, or if their root systems are substantially developed, they may be set directly into the garden.

8: Pots of rooted azalea cuttings are stored in a coldframe during the winter months. Plants in the garden should also be protected.

Herman Gantner

the country. Tree seeds such as acorns, buckeyes, elm or red maple seed may be planted.

Dogwood, persimmon, Juneberry, sweet gum, yellowwood or tulip tree seed will have to be stratified. Stratifying means storing the seed in moist sand, soil or sawdust at temperatures above freezing. Some seed is improved by freezing, however. It can be gathered in fall and stored over winter. Among these are seed of golden rain tree, yellowwood, flowering dogwood and redbud.

30

Propagating with Hardwood Cuttings

KENNETH MEYER

MANY deciduous shrubs and some trees can be easily propagated from hardwood cuttings taken in fall. This method has been successful to start dozens of mockoranges, several specimens of *Deutzia gracilis*, a white wistaria and two Concord grapevines, to name a few.

October and November are the best months for taking hardwood cuttings. Generally speaking, it is well to wait until after a few frosts, when the plants have dropped their leaves and become dormant.

The cuttings are taken from healthy stems or canes of the current season's growth. Each should be seven to nine inches long and of approximately lead-pencil thickness, with at least three or four buds or nodes (leaf joints).

The base of each cutting should be cut straight across and just below a node. The tip usually is cut off on a slant, so it will be easy to distinguish from the base later on. Exceptions are rose of Sharon and weigela, which should be propagated from tip cuttings. The basal part of each stem is best discarded, as it is usually too hard and thick to root readily.

Cuttings of each kind of shrub are tied with soft wire or tarred string in separate bundles of ten to twenty-five each. The butt ends are kept together. Be sure to attach a weatherproof identifying label to each bundle. Thus prepared, the cuttings are ready for winter storage; during this time they form calluses (protective tissue on the cut surfaces) which are conducive to root formation the following spring.

The bundles of cuttings may be buried in a coldframe. Equally good is a deep box filled with slightly damp soil, sand or sawdust; the box is stored in an outbuilding or unheated cellar where the temperature remains around 40 to 45 degrees. The material around the cuttings should not be too moist. It should neither exude water nor absorb vital moisture from the cuttings. It must not be allowed to freeze.

A simpler way to handle hardwood cuttings is to bury them below the frost line in a well-drained garden location where there is no danger of standing water. A trench is dug deeply enough to accommodate the bundles standing vertically (with butt ends up). Horizontal storage is satisfactory, too. To insure good drainage, a layer of coarse sand about two inches thick is spread over the bottom.

After the cuttings are in place, sandy soil is used to fill in the trench and form a mound over it to a height of a foot or more. With the approach of severe weather, pile a thick mulch of straw, salt hay or litter on top of the mound; this will further help to preclude temperature fluctuation caused by the sun. Such insulation is also a wise precaution when a coldframe is used as the storage place. A labeled stake driven into the ground at each end of the trench will serve to mark the spot; otherwise it is difficult to locate the cuttings in spring.

Nothing more need be done until spring, except to prepare the ground in the intended garden site so it will be ready for spring planting. The soil should be spaded deeply, left rough, and allowed to settle over winter.

In April or May, when the soil is dry enough to be worked, it should be hoed, raked, and made ready for planting the same as any other garden bed. The best way to plant the cuttings is to dig a narrow trench at least seven inches deep, with one side nearly vertical and the other sloping.

Do not use chemical fertilizer, but mix liberal quantities of humus or screened compost into the trench. To be on the safe side, place an inch-deep layer of sand in the bottom for good drainage.

Space the cuttings, butt ends down, six or eight inches apart against the vertical side of the trench. The tip of each cutting should be only a couple of inches above the ground. Fill in with good sandy soil and tamp it firmly around the base of each cutting. Leave a slight depression to catch rain water.

Do not let the cuttings dry out while the planting is in progress. The callus is soft and dries quickly when exposed. Wrap the cuttings in a damp cloth while working.

There is some difference of opinion about treating the cuttings with a root-inducing hormone before planting. Some gardeners have found it unnecessary, but such treatment might be of considerable value with hard-to-root species. The chemicals are available in various strengths. A simple test can be conducted by treating a portion of the cuttings and then checking the rooting results against the untreated cuttings.

Once planted, the cuttings require no special attention beyond shallow cultivation and a good watering twice a week in really dry weather. By the end of the first growing season most of the cuttings will have developed into husky plants, one to three feet tall, with two or three stems.

Among the many popular plants which may be propagated easily from hardwood cuttings are beautybush (*Kolkwitzia amabilis*), cotoneaster, shrubby honeysuckle, kerria, forsythia, flowering quince, elaeagnus and certain spireas. The viburnums are also good plants for rooting this way, as are euonymus, currants, gooseberries, climbing roses and trumpet vines.

3 1

Protection Against Plant Troubles

DANIEL DOWD

BEAUTY in the garden is better retained by avoidance of trouble rather than by arduous recovery efforts. Good soil, vigorous plants and proper attention to water and nutrients give the garden a good start. Poorly adapted plants or trouble-prone varieties are to be avoided. Poor sanitation invites trouble, and insects come uninvited. Regular application of preventive sprays wards off problems and checks the build-up of uninvited insects. Foliar feeding, easily combined with sprays, corrects nutritional deficiencies.

Before a plant trouble can be effectively treated, it must be properly recognized and identified. Similar symptoms might result from a variety of things such as insects, diseases, root damage or poor nutrition. Intrinsic symptoms are only vague indications of a disease; yellowing leaves, for example, may result from a dozen causes. Extrinsic signs, however, are definite evidence of a specific, recognizable trouble; such signs may be a fungous growth or a pattern of destruction made by a chewing insect.

When the trouble is defined, the proper remedy can be sought. Information in bulletins, handbooks and texts on plant diseases and insects will aid identification. Competent nurserymen, garden center personnel and extension service people can often help with the identification of plant troubles and recommend corrective measures. Home gardeners can also learn valuable pointers from short courses and garden lectures.

Safe Use of Garden Chemicals

SERIOUS insect and disease problems are controlled quickly with specially compounded sprays and dusts. Some materials are applied directly to the plant stems and foliage. Others are applied to the soil, including fumigants, drenches, dusts and granular materials. The results of such measures justify the means, and for this reason some chemical controls will always be a part of gardening. The careful person can handle these materials wisely if he has a good knowledge of their proper and safe use.

STORAGE

Do not store chemicals near foodstuffs.
Keep them locked in cabinets or on high shelves beyond the reach of children.
Store them in their original containers.
Destroy empty containers.

USE AND HANDLING

Use low toxicity products.
Avoid breathing of fumes; stay out of the drift.
Use a respirator mask if possible.
Avoid direct contact with materials; wear rubber gloves and protective clothing.
Wash thoroughly after using the materials and especially before eating.

APPLICATION

READ THE DIRECTIONS ON THE PACKAGE.
Follow recommended dilutions.
Spray the under sides of leaves thoroughly.
Check to see that both surfaces are evenly wetted.
Avoid foliage injury—do not spray in high temperatures.

EMERGENCY MEASURES

Check precautions on the package.

Post the location and telephone number of the nearest poison control center.

Post first aid directions.

A safe combination of materials for an all-purpose garden spray could contain: sevin for insects; malathion for insects and some mites; kelthane for mites; captan for leaf diseases. For fruit plants: methoxychlor or lindane, malathion, kelthane or tedion, captan. For vegetables: sevin, rotenone, captan.

Chemical Control of Insects and Pests

INSECTS are typed according to the manner in which they feed upon plants. Control measures are designed to destroy them during the most vulnerable period of their life cycle. In the dormant season, stronger materials can be used to kill eggs and scale insects without danger of foliage injury. Included in this category are some pests which are not true insects—mites, slugs and nematodes.

There are four types of insects and pests: chewing, sucking, boring and subterranean. Chewing insects attack the exposed parts of plants and can be poisoned by substances applied to the plant surfaces.

Sucking insects draw juices from within the plants by piercing; these may be controlled by insecticides that kill on contact. They are also controlled with systematic poisons dissolved in the plant sap.

Boring and tunneling insects get within a plant and, once there, are difficult to control by ordinary means.

Subterranean or soil pests may feed by any of the above methods, but they are difficult to detect and require control measures that include soil sterilization, treatment of the soil with stomach poisons and drenching the soil with contact insecticides.

Control of Insects and Pests

COMMON CHEWING INSECTS

Insect	Control
Grasshopper	DDT, chlordane
Caterpillars and "worms" (smooth-skinned moth larvae)	Chlordane, lead arsenate
Beetles	DDT, lead arsenate, chlordane

Hornets	Chlordane, DDT
Maggots (larvae of flies)	Malathion, chlordane
Slugs and snails (slimy, night-feeding mollusks)	Metaldehyde bait

Common Piercing-sucking Insects

Insect	Control
Aphids (plant lice)	Nicotine sulfate, malathion, lindane
Leafhoppers	Malathion
Chinch bugs	Chlordane dust, malathion spray
White flies	Malathion
Scale insects	Dormant: lime-sulfur, miscible oil. Active: superior oil on some woody shrubs, malathion on young crawlers during summer
Mealy bugs	Malathion
Plant bugs	Malathion

Rasping-sucking Insects

Insect	Control
Thrips	Pyrethrin, DDT, malathion, lindane

Boring and Mining Insects

Insect	Control
Leaf miners (larvae of moths and beetles; certain adult beetles)	DDT, dieldrin; prune and burn affected parts
Foliar nematodes	Propagate plants from clean stock
Borers	Paint or spray bark with DDT. Cut out borers or skewer holes with wire; push fumigant pastes into borings

Subterranean Pests

Grubs (larvae of beetles)	Lead arsenate, chlordane, or dieldrin mixed into the soil
Moles	Grubproofing reduces natural food of moles and they go elsewhere
Nematodes	Fumigation of soil before planting. Root treatment with VC13 or Nemagon
Ants and termites	Chlordane

Control of Pests and Diseases of Needled Evergreens

Host plant	Symptom	Sign	Pest (causative agent)	Control
Abies (fir)	Needles redden		Twig blight	Prune out; copper fungicide
	Curled needles and dying shoots	White wax	Aphids	Malathion, lindane
	Defoliation	2″ to 3″ sacs	Bagworm	Lead arsenate, malathion
	Yellowing needles	Fine webbing; minute crawlers	Spider mite	Lime-sulfur, kelthane, dimite
Cedrus (true cedar)	Branch dieback	Tiny, black fruiting bodies	Tip blight	Prune out; copper fungicide
	Leaders die	Grubs in wood	Tip weevil	Malathion, DDT in spring
Cryptomeria	Twigs brown		Leaf blight	Prune out; copper fungicide
	Foliage brown on west side		Wind burn	
	General browning		Oilspray injury	Use no oil on genus
Chamaecyparis (plume cypress)		Witches broom	Fungus	Prune out and burn
Picea (spruce)	Lower branches dead	Small resinous cankers	Fungus	Prune out; copper fungicide
	Pineapplelike galls	Aphids on tip galls	Spruce gall aphid	Prune out; spray in March with malathion
	Foliage thinned and ragged	Caterpillars	Caterpillars	Lead aresnate, malathion
	Yellow needles	Fine webbing	Spider mite	(See Abies)
	Shoot dieback; bleeding	Small borers	White pine weevil	(See Pinus)
	Dieback	Streaky wood	Tip blight	Prune out; copper fungicide
	Dying branches	Blistered bark	White pine blister rust	Spray actidione; eradicate currants and gooseberries
	White cottony patches	Cottony aphids	Bark aphid	Lindane, malathion
	Needles chewed	Green larvae	Sawfly	Lead arsenate, methoxychlor

Host plant	Symptom	Sign	Pest (*causative agent*)	Control
	Needles bunched in tubes	Green or brown larvae	Tube moth	Lead arsenate, methoxychlor
	Tips webbed, sawdust present	Striped larvae	Spruce web-worm	Malathion, methoxychlor
	Wilting new shoots	White cater-pillar	White pine tip moth	Prune and burn
	Damaged shoots	Resin masses	European pine shoot moth	Hand pick; methoxychlor
Taxus (yew)	Small dead twigs	none	none	Ice damage
	Winter loss	none	Drainage	Correct soil condition
	Yellowing leaves; partial dieback	Roots and leaves chewed	Taxus vine weevil	Spray base of plants with chlordane or dieldrin
	Sooty honeydew on foliage	White, waxy branches	Taxus mealy bug	Malathion in June
Tsuga (hemlock)	Needle fall	Brown scale on leaf bottoms	Fiorinia scale	Dimethoate
	Needle fall	Gray scale	Aspidiotus scale	Malathion in August
	Yellow leaves	Fine webbing	Spider mite	Kelthane, aramite
	Bagworm		Bagworm	Malathion lead arsenate

Broadleaved Evergreens

Host Plant	Symptom	Sign	Pest	Control
Azalea	Watery collapse flowers	Small fruiting bodies on the ground (sclerotia)	Petal blight	Parzate spray; pick off dead flowers
	Leaves mottled; edges rolled	Small green, later white, winged in-sect	White fly	Malathion
	Leaves bronzy	Tobacco stain spots on underside of foliage	Lacebug	Malathion
Buxus (boxwood)	Dead branches, peeling bark	Orange-pink fruiting bodies	Nectria canker	Prune; fertilize; copper fungi-cide

Host Plant	Symptom	Sign	Pest	Control
	Leaves russeted	Sun scald	Winter injury	Mulch; protect from wind; use anti-desiccants
	Dwarfing; bronzing of foliage; die-back	None	Nematodes	Nemagon
	Leaves clipped	Small green flies	Psyllid	Malathion, lin-dane
Euonymus	Defoliation; dieback	White scales	Various scales	Elgetol in spring; mala-thion in sum-mer
	Stem galls		Gall bacteria	Prune out
Hedera (ivy)			Several insect pests	Malathion
Ilex (holly)	Leaf spots			Burn old leaves; ferbam, cap-tan
	Leaf blotches	Larval tunnels	Leaf miners	Lindane, diel-drin
Kalmia (mountain laurel)	Leaf spots		Fungus	Ferbam, captan
Pieris (andro-meda)	Leaves bronzed	Dark spots under leaf	Lacebug	Malathion, diel-drin
	Leaves bronzed	Fine web under foliage	Spider mite	Kelthane, ara-mite
Rhododen-dron	Leaves yel-lowed	Darker color along main veins	Chlorosis	Check soil acid-ity; use iron chelates
	Leaves browned		Winter or drought injury	Mulch; screen from winds; use anti-desiccants
	Wilting; die-back of older branches	Holes in stems	Borers	Prune; fertilize; paint stems with DDT
			Spider mite	Kelthane; ara-mite
			Aphids; leaf-hoppers	Malathion

3 2

Diagnosis of Tree Troubles

DANIEL DOWD

TREES prosper when standard practices of soil aeration, watering, fertilization and proper pruning are followed. When troubles do occur, the blame can not always be attributed to insect damage or disease. Poor drainage, poor soil, compacted soil and undersized planting pockets are common reasons for poor tree growth. Abnormal climate—excessively wet or dry, hot or cold weather—may cause or intensify such troubles as leaf diseases, leaf scorch, sunscald and frost cracks. In other cases, chemical injury, gas leakage, girdled roots may be hidden reasons for poor tree vigor. Where symptoms are confused, the advice of a trained arborist or horticulturist is valuable.

General Pests

APHIDS (plant lice), spider mites, scale insects and caterpillars attack a wide variety of trees. They multiply rapidly and damage from their great number reduces tree vigor. Weakened trees are a prey to borer attack, diseases and winter injury. Dormant sprays control aphids before they can increase and cause serious damage. When leaf-eating insects appear (cankerworms, beetles, tent caterpillars), they are easily combatted with contact sprays or stomach poisons such as sevin, methoxychlor, lead arsenate or DDT.

Control of Tree Troubles

Host Plant	Symptom	Sign	Pest (causative agent)	Control
Acer (maple)	Sudden wilt, withering and dying leaves and branches	Stained sapwood; green streaks at margin of stain	Verticillium (fungus)	Prune diseased branches; fertilize and water; cover pruning cuts with wound paint

NOTE: Nearly all deciduous trees are infected by this disease, but maples are most susceptible.

Host Plant	Symptom	Sign	Pest (causative agent)	Control
		Sticky leaves and honey-dew on parked cars; aphids on leaves	Aphids	Malathion or lindane
Aesculus (horse-chestnut)	Blotched and browned leaves	Tiny black specks in centers of blotches	Guignardia (fungus)	Burn fallen leaves; spray captan or ziram two or more times in early spring
	Browning of tree on sunny and windy side	Margins of leaves brown and curl	Leaf scorch (environ-mental)	Water trees thoroughly in dry seasons; apply fer-tilizer
Albizzia (silk tree)	Wilting and dy-ing of leaves; dark ring stain in outer sapwood		Fusarium (soil-borne fungus)	Select disease-resistant plants; no control known
	Leaves bunched together and skeletonized	Gray and white striped lar-vae, ½" long	Webworm	Malathion or lead arsenate
Betula (birch)	Browning of spring foliage	Tunnels and larvae within the leaves	Birch leaf miner	Spray new foliage with lindane or dieldrin
	Dead and dying upper branches	White larvae boring in branches	Bronze birch borer	Dieldrin or DDT in June; keep trees in good vigor
Catalpa	Gray foliage in summer		Powdery mil-dew	Karathan or sul-fur
Celtis (hack-berry)	Tight clusters of short twigs		Witches broom	Prune and burn; dormant spray (lime sulfur)
Cercis (redbud)	Sunken areas of bark; dying or girdled branches		Canker	Prune out affected branches; ex-cise main lesions

Host Plant	Symptom	Sign	Pest (causative agent)	Control
Cornus (dogwood)	Unthrifty appearance; drooping, discolored, undersized leaves	Sunken canker at base of trunk; bark and wood discolored	Crown canker	Repair small cankers; avoid bark injuries
		Dead bark on side exposed to sun and drying winds	Sunscald	Protect from excessive drying; cut away dead bark; apply wound dressing
	Dying branches	Shot holes in bark and borers under bark	Borers	Keep plants in good vigor; paint bark with a slurry of DDT or dieldrin
	Spotted and decayed floral bracts		Botrytis blight (fungus)	Spray zineb in April; continue monthly until midsummer
Crataegus (hawthorn)	Leaves scorched and browned	Bark blackened and peeling	Fire blight (bacterial)	Prune out and burn; spray streptomycin
	Premature leaf fall	Small leaf spots	Leaf blight (fungus)	Zineb or actidione; burn fallen leaves
Fagus (beech)	Dead bark	Fluffy white scale bodies	Bark disease; woolly beech scale	Feeding scale insects expose bark to fungus attack; dormant lime sulfur and summer spray of malathion controls the insect
Fraxinus (ash)	Weakened growth and dieback of tops		Poor growing conditions	Keep trees healthy and vigorous by applying fertilizer; water and soil aeration

Host Plant	Symptom	Sign	Pest (causative agent)	Control
Gleditsia (honey locust)	Leaves distorted and podlike	Small larvae inside pod	Podgall midge	Lindane or malathion
	Leaves clustered and webbed together	Larvae between leaves	Webworm	Sevin, lindane or malathion
Liriodendron (tuliptree)	Sunken areas in bark		Canker	Prune and burn affected branches
	Dying branches; sooty mold on leaves	Soft, brown turtle-shaped scales on twigs	Tulip scale	Dormant spray (miscible oil); summer spray malathion
Magnolia		Several kinds of scales occur		Dormant spray (miscible oil); summer spray malathion
Malus (flowering apple; crabapple)	NOTE: There are about thirty common troubles of apple trees. Ornamental apples are subject to the same. Special bulletins by state agricultural services are recommended.			
Platanus (plane tree or sycamore)	Dying and browning of leaves in early spring	Sunken cankers on small twigs	Anthracnose (fungus)	Burn fallen twigs and leaves; spray fixed copper or phenyl mercury compounds or captan several times during wet springs
	Foliage thin and undersized; yellow and falling; elongated cankers on trunk and branches	Wood is deeply stained reddish-brown	Ceratocystis canker stain fungus	No known cure; remove infected trees; sterilize pruning tools and wound paint brushes to prevent spread
	Browning and falling of inner leaves during dry weather		Drought	Deep-water trees
Quercus (oak)	Leaves blotched; deformed in early spring		Anthracnose (fungus)	(See Platanus)

Host Plant	Symptom	Sign	Pest (causative agent)	Control
	Foliage yellow (pin oaks)		Chlorosis	Check soil pH; should be acid; treat with iron chelates or ferrous sulfate
	Weak growth; dying twigs	Budlike scales in leaf axils	Kermes scale	Dormant miscible oil; malathion in leaf stage
	Tiny shrunken pits in smooth bark	Greenish gold scales	Golden oak scale	(same as above)
Robinia (black locust)	Dead upper branches in otherwise vigorous trees	Borers girdling the branches	Locust tree borer	Spray trunk and branches with dieldrin

NOTE: Borers open the tree to attack by wood-destroying fungi which cannot be controlled.

Salix (willow)	Spring foliage wilts and blackens; cankers on twigs		Leaf blight	Fixed-copper spray; prune dead branches; plant resistant species

NOTE: Willows require abundant moisture and cannot thrive in dry soils. Weak trees are subject to borer attack for which dieldrin is recommended. Canker, scale and other insect attacks are common requiring frequent control.

Ulmus (elm)	Sudden wilting and death of branches	Brown stain in new growth rings	Dutch elm disease (fungus)	No known cure; remove infected trees.

NOTE: While other diseases attack elms, the epidemic nature of the Dutch elm disease constitutes a major threat. Preventive programs are the chief means of preserving elms. Community wide measures are more effective than individual efforts. Elm bark beetles carry the disease to trees in weakened condition. Prompt removal of dead elms and pruning of dead branches reduces breeding places. Heavy dormant spraying of specimen trees gives a good measure of protection against adult beetles which feed in tree tops during the summer. Applications of fertilizer and deep watering in dry periods insure tree vigor.

33

Catalogue of Trees and Shrubs

JOAN LEE FAUST

THE majority of plants mentioned here were chosen for their decorative features at different seasons. Some species were included to meet the needs of "problem areas." Individual specimens can be used as accents, or groupings of plants can be arranged to complete a landscape feature. All of these plants should be available from quality nurseries.

Hedge Plants

(E—evergreen; D—deciduous *—tall hedge)

INFORMAL

Abelia grandiflora (glossy abelia): D
Acanthopanax sieboldianus: D
Chaenomeles japonica (Japanese quince): D
Euonymus alatus compactus (burning bush): D
Hibiscus syriacus (rose of Sharon): D
Philadelphus species (mockorange): D
Rosa species (rose):D
Taxus species (yew): E
Tsuga canadensis (Canadian hemlock): E
Syringa species (lilac): D

FORMAL

Berberis julianae (wintergreen barberry): E
Buxus species (boxwood): E
Carpinus betulus (European hornbeam): D

Cornus mas (Cornelian cherry): D
Ilex species (holly): E
Ligustrum species (privet): D
Picea abies (dwarf Norway spruce): E
Poncirus trifoliata (hardy orange): D
Pyracantha species (firethorn): D
Salix purpurea (dwarf willow): D

Groundcovers

(H—herbaceous; E—evergreen; D—deciduous)

FOR SHADE

Ajuga reptans (bugle): H
Convallaria majalis (lily of the valley): H
Epimedium grandiflorum: H
Hedera helix (English ivy): E
Hypericum calycinum (Aaron's beard St. Johnswort): E
Mitchella repens (partridgeberry): E
Pachistma canbyi: E
Pachysandra species (spurge): E
Vinca minor (myrtle): E
Xanthorhiza simplicissima (yellowroot): D

FOR SUN

Ajuga reptans (bugle): H
Arctostaphylos uva-ursi (bearberry): E
Campanula carpatica (Carpathian bellflower): H
Cerastium tomentosum (snow-in-summer): H
Cotoneaster dammeri (bearberry cotoneaster):E
Euonymus fortunei (wintercreeper): E
Hedera helix (English ivy): E
Juniperus species (juniper): E
Phlox divaricata (sweet-william phlox): H
Phlox subulata (moss pink): H
Potentilla tridentata (wineleaf cinquefoil): E
Rosa Max Graf: D
Sedum species: H
Thymus serpyllum (creeping thyme): E
Vinca minor (myrtle): E
Viola species (violets): H

Low Shrubbery

(under 3 feet)

Chaenomeles japonica (flowering quince): showy flowers in early May; red, white or pink varieties; easily grown

Cotoneaster horizontalis (rock spray): flat habit desirable for hugging rocks and groundcover; bright red berries ornamental in fall

Daphne cneorum (rose daphne): cunning shrub with fragrant pink-red flowers; requires winter protection in northern climates

Euonymus fortunei (glossy wintercreeper): glossy evergreen foliage; showy red berries in fall; requires spraying to control scale

Ilex crenata varieties (Japanese holly): excellent evergreen for many landscaping purposes; small, rounded leaves; hardy to Zone 6

Juniperus sabina tamariscifolia (Savin juniper): blue-green foliage, ornamental habit; easily grown

Rhododendron species: innumerable fine selections in the clan for ornamental use

Spiraea bumalda Anthony Waterer (spirea): long-blooming dwarf shrub

Viburnum opulus nanum (European cranberry-bush): flat clusters of white flowers in May; autumn color; non-fruiting

Medium-Height Shrubbery

(4 to 6 feet)

Abelia grandiflora (glossy abelia): showy pink flowers in late summer; glossy foliage; grows in full sun or modest shade

Berberis julianae (wintergreen barberry): spiny ornamental foliage; yellow blooms followed by blue-black berries in fall; hardy and durable

Deutzia gracilis (slender deutzia): graceful habit with arching stems; white flowers in late May; hardy

Ilex crenata species (Japanese holly): excellent evergreen for landscaping; glossy foliage; hardy to Zone 6

Juniperus squamata meyeri (Meyer's juniper): blue-toned evergreen foliage; ornamental habit; hardy

Kerria japonica (kerria): showy flowers in mid-May; needs pruning to retain its symmetry; green winter twigs

Leucothoe catesbaei (drooping leucothoe): requires acid soil; semi-evergreen foliage turns bronze in fall; hardy

Mahonia aquifolium (Oregon holly grape): shiny, dark evergreen foliage; yellow flowers in May followed by blue-black fruits; foliage does become windburned in exposed locations

Pieris japonica (Japanese andromeda): glossy, evergreen foliage; pendant clusters of bell-like blooms in early spring; durable shrub, prefers acid soil

Pinus mugo compacta (Mugo pine): dwarf compact pine for foundation planting; hardy and durable

Potentilla fruticosa (cinquefoil): showy yellow flowers throughout summer; very hardy

Rhododendron species: innumerable selections in the clan for ornamental use

Spiraea salicifolia (willowleaf spirea): upright habit; unusual foliage; blooms in July

Taxus species: many varieties and hybrids available

Viburnum tomentosum (doublefile viburnum): handsome flowers borne on horizontal branches; red berries in fall; hardy

Shrubs for Shade

Abelia grandiflora (glossy abelia): hardy; pink flowers in late summer; excellent foliage

Berberis thunbergi (Japanese barberry): thorny twigs; rugged grower; fall foliage and fruit color

Camellia japonica: where hardy, excellent broadleaved evergreen with showy flowers; prefers northern exposure

Clethra alnifolia (summersweet): fragrant spikes of bloom in summer; needs room to spread; prefers moist, acid soil

Cornus stolonifera (red osier dogwood): bright orange-red twigs; requires moist soil and renewal pruning

Forsythia species: early spring flowers; trouble-free; vigorous shrub; pruning required to keep it in proper shape

Hamamelis species (witch hazel): late fall or early spring floral display; dense shrub; hardy

Kalmia latifolia (mountain laurel): handsome evergreen; showy June flowers; acid soil

Leucothoe catesbaei (drooping leucothoe): long waxy foliage; June bloom; acid soil

Lonicera species (honeysuckle): rugged grower; fragrant summer bloom followed by showy fall berries

Mahonia aquifolium (Oregon holly-grape): waxy, hollylike foliage; showy yellow flowers in May followed by ornamental fruits

Pieris species (andromeda): dark, evergreen foliage; pendant white blooms in early spring; excellent landscape shrub for acid soil

Rhododendron species: excellent ornamentals for moist, acid soil

Taxus species (yew): sturdy, needled evergreens for assorted land-scape use; spray for weevil control

Viburnum species: large shrubs with showy ornamental flowers in summer followed by colorful fruit

Shrubs for Berry Display

Aronia arbutifolia (red chokeberry): red
Berberis species (barberry): red
Callicarpa japonica (beautyberry): purple
Cotoneaster species: red
Ilex species (holly): black and red
Ligustrum species (privet): black
Lonicera species (honeysuckle): bright red
Mahonia aquifolium (Oregon holly-grape): blue-black
Nandina domestica (semi-hardy): purple-red
Pyracantha species (firethorn): orange
Rosa rugosa (rose): red
Symphoricarpos orbiculatus (coralberry): purple-red
Viburnum species: purple-red

Shrubs for Fall Color

Aronia arbutifolia (red chokeberry): red
Berberis species (barberry): red
Clethra alnifolia (summer sweet): yellow-orange
Enkianthus campanulatus (redvein enkianthus): bright red
Euonymus alatus compactus (burning bush): red
Fothergilla major: yellow to red
Hamamelis species (witch hazel): yellow
Leucothoe catesbaei (drooping leucothoe): bronze
Mahonia aquifolium (Oregon holly-grape): bronze
Spiraea prunifolia (bridalwreath spirea): red-orange
Viburnum species: red to purple

Trees for Fall Color

Acer species (maple): red to orange-yellow
Amelanchier canadensis (shadbush): red to bright yellow
Carpinus caroliniana (American hornbeam): orange-red
Cercis canadensis (eastern redbud): yellow
Cladrastis lutea (yellowwood): yellow
Cornus species (dogwood): red
Liquidambar styraciflua (sweet gum): scarlet
Nyssa sylvatica (black gum): red-orange
Quercus species (oak): red-purple to russet-orange

List of Authors

AVERY, DR. GEORGE S., JR.: Director of the Brooklyn Botanic Garden, pioneer in plant-hormone studies

BAUMGARTNER, DR. L. L.: Director of Baumlanda Horticultural Research Laboratories, Croton Falls, New York

BROOKS, MAURICE: Professor of Wildlife Management, West Virginia University, with special interests in woody plants, ferns and birds

CAPEN, BARBARA M: landscape architect and resident of Long Island with special interests in perennials and better ornamentals

CHIDAMIAN, CLAUDE: author of *Camellias for Everyone* and *Bonsai-Miniature Trees*

CLARK, ROBERT B.: Senior Curator, Liberty Hyde Bailey Hortorium, Ithaca, New York

DENGLER, HARRY W.: Extension Forester, University of Maryland

DOWD, DANIEL: Associate Professor, Department of Ornamental Horticulture, Long Island Agricultural and Technical Institute, Farmingdale, New York

DUDA, DR. EDWARD J.: Director, Bartlett Tree Experts, Stamford, Connecticut

ENGEL, DAVID H.: landscape architect and author of *Japanese Gardens for Today*

GOLDMAN, ALAN W.: advertising copywriter and consultant on azaleas and rhododendrons

IREYS, ALICE R.: landscape architect in Long Island-Westchester County area

KORBOBO, RAYMOND P.: Assistant Professor, Department of Horticulture, Rutgers University

LEACH, DAVID G.: author of *Rhododendrons of the World*

LEUTHARDT, HENRY P.: nurseryman specializing in espalier, Portchester, New York

LEWIS, CLARENCE E.: Associate Professor, Department of Horticulture, Michigan State University

MEYER, KENNETH: amateur gardener specializing in woody plants and perennials

PAINE, BARBARA B.: wild-flower hobbyist and free-lance writer

ROCKWELL, F. F.: co-author with Mrs. Rockwell of many books including *The Complete Book of Bulbs, The Complete Book of Roses, The Complete Book of Lawns;* Garden Editor, *The New York Times,* 1933-43

RUSDEN, DR. PHILIP J.: Pathologist, Bartlett Tree Experts, Stamford, Connecticut

SAMPLE, MARJORIE: amateur gardener, co-operating with the American Camellia Society, on cold-hardiness studies

THOMASSON, R. R.: former Assistant Director of the Cooperative Extension Service, University of Missouri; hobbies are gardening, nature, photography and free-lance writing

VOS, DR. FRANCIS DE: Assistant Director, National Arboretum, Washington, D. C.

Sources of Plants and Supplies

The following list consists mainly of firms that sell directly to individual customers by mail and issue annual catalogues. There are modest charges for some of these catalogues.

FRUITS

Kelly Brothers Nurseries, Inc.
Dansville, New York 14437

Henry Leuthardt (espalier)
Port Chester, New York 10573

New York State Fruit Testing Cooperative Assoc.
Geneva, New York 14456

Stark Brothers Nurseries
Louisiana, Missouri 63353

GARDENING SUPPLIES

Gardener's Cupboard
P. O. Box 61
12 Points Station
Terre Haute, Indiana 47804

House Plant Corner
P. O. Box 810
Oxford, Maryland 21654

Max Schling Seedsmen, Inc.
538 Madison Avenue
New York, New York 10022

Vaughan's Seed Company
24 Vesey Street
New York, New York 10007

SEED

Breck's
250 Breck Building
Boston, Massachusetts 02110

Joseph Harris Seed Company
Rochester, New York 14611

Burnett Brothers, Inc.
92 Chambers Street
New York, New York 10007

Burnett-Seedsmen, Inc.
23-25 Warren Street
New York, New York 10017

W. Atlee Burpee Company
Philadelphia, Pennsylvania 19132

George W. Park Seed Company
Greenwood, South Carolina 29646

Harry E. Saier (rare)
Dimondale, Michigan 48821

TREES AND SHRUBS

Bay State Nurseries
Monponsett Street
Halifax, Massachusetts 02238

Corliss Brothers
Reynard Street
Gloucester, Massachusetts 01930

Earle Dilatush (holly)
R.F.D. #1
Robbinsville, New Jersey 08552

Kingsville Nursery
Kingsville, Maryland 21087

Oliver & Simson Nurseries, Inc.
   (azaleas and rhododendrons)
313 Central Avenue
Scarsdale, New York 10584

Rosedale Nurseries
Millbrook, New York
Hawthorne, New York 10532

Stern's Nurseries
Geneva, New York 14456

Tingle Nursery Company
Pittsville, Maryland 21850

Weston Nursery, Inc.
Hopkinton, Massachusetts 01748

Further Reading

GENERAL REFERENCES

Bush-Brown, Louise and James: *America's Garden Book*. New York: Charles Scribner's Sons; 1958.
Everett, T. H. (ed.): *The New Illustrated Encyclopedia of Gardening*. New York: Greystone Press; 1960. Six volumes.

TAYLOR, NORMAN (ed.): *Taylor's Encyclopedia of Gardening*. Boston: Houghton Mifflin Company; 1961.

WESTCOTT, CYNTHIA: *The Gardener's Bug Book*. Garden City, N.Y.: Doubleday & Company; 1956.

LANDSCAPING

BUSHEY, DONALD J.: *A Guide to Home Landscaping*. New York: McGraw-Hill Book Company; 1956.

DUSTAN, ALICE L.: *Landscaping Your Own Home*. New York: The Macmillan Company; 1955.

LEES, CARLTON B.: *Budget Landscaping*. New York: Henry Holt & Company; 1960.

MALKIN, ROBERT: *How To Landscape Your Own Home*. New York: Harper & Brothers; 1955.

MORSE, HARRIET K.: *Gardening in the Shade*. Revised edition. New York: Charles Scribner's Sons; 1962.

TREES, SHRUBS AND VINES

CHIDAMIAN, CLAUDE: *Camellias for Everyone*. Garden City, N.Y.: Doubleday & Company; 1959.

CLARKE, J. HAROLD: *Getting Started with Rhododendrons and Azaleas*. Garden City, N.Y.: Doubleday & Company; 1960.

GRAVES, ARTHUR HARMOUNT: *Illustrated Guide to Trees and Shrubs*. Revised edition. New York: Harper & Brothers; 1950.

HALLER, JOHN M.: *Tree Care*. New York: The Macmillan Company; 1957

HOWARD, FRANCES: *Landscaping with Vines*. New York: The Macmillan Company; 1959.

HUME, H. H.: *Camellias, Kinds and Culture*. New York: The Macmillan Company; 1951.

————: *Hollies*. New York: The Macmillan Company; 1953.

LEE, FREDERICK P.: *The Azalea Book*. Princeton, N.J.: D. Van Nostrand Company; 1958.

WYMAN, DONALD: *Ground Cover Plants*. New York: The Macmillan Company; 1956.

————: *Shrubs and Vines for American Gardens*. New York: The Macmillan Company; 1949.

————: *Trees for American Gardens*. New York: The Macmillan Company; 1956.

YOSHIMURA, YUJI, AND HALFORD, G. M.: *The Japanese Art of Miniature Trees and Landscapes*. Rutland, Vt.: Charles E. Tuttle Co., 1957.

LAWNS

CARLETON, R. MILTON: *Your Lawn: How to Make It and Keep It*. Princeton, N.J.: D. Van Nostrand Company; 1959.

SCHERY, ROBERT W.: *The Lawn Book*. New York: The Macmillan Company; 1961.

Index

A NOTE ON THE TYPE

THE TEXT of this book is set in *Caledonia,* a Linotype
face designed by W. A. DWIGGINS, the man responsible
for so much that is good in contemporary book design
and typography. Caledonia belongs to the family of
printing types called "modern face" by printers—a
term used to mark the change in style of type-letters
that occurred about 1800. Caledonia borders on the
general design of Scotch Modern but is more freely
drawn than that letter.

Composed and bound by H. Wolff, New York
Printed by Halliday Lithograph Corporation,
West Hanover, Massachusetts